Between Ordinary and Extraordinary

Art and Law

Volumes published in this Brill Research Perspectives title are listed at *brill.com/rpal*

Between Ordinary and Extraordinary

The Normativity of the Singular Case in Art and Law

By

Angela Condello

BRILL

LEIDEN | BOSTON

This publication went through a process of double peer review.

This paperback book edition is simultaneously published as issue 2.1 (2018) of *Art and Law*, DOI 10.1163/24684309-12340003.

Library of Congress Control Number: 2018945237

Typeface for the Latin, Greek, and Cyrillic scripts: "Brill". See and download: brill.com/brill-typeface.

ISBN 978-90-04-38130-8 (paperback)
ISBN 978-90-04-38131-5 (e-book)

This book is printed on acid-free paper and produced in a sustainable manner.

For Tiziano and Leonardo

Contents

Between Ordinary and Extraordinary

The Normativity of the Singular Case in Art and Law

Angela Condello
University of Turin, Italy
angela.condello@unito.it

Abstract

What is the relationship between the general, abstract norm and the singular, concrete case that sometimes affirms a parallel, contrasting, norm? The present book engages with this question. The argument stems from an analysis of extraordinary singular cases that sometimes emerge, sometimes are "produced" or "promoted" as exemplary (for strategic reasons, like in law). I argue that approaching normativity in art and law from the perspective of the singular case also illustrates the theoretical importance of interdisciplinary legal scholarship, since the singularity creates room for extra-legal values to emerge as legitimate demands, desires, needs.

Keywords

singularity – extraordinary – ordinary – exemplary jurisprudential case – exemplary artwork – normativity – genre – law – art – norm – normative order

Introduction

The idea for this book emerged during the International Roundtable for the Semiotics of Law that took place at Cardozo Law School and New York University in 2017. The Roundtable was organized by Peter Goodrich and myself and its theme was the normativity of singularity in law. On the last day, during the conclusive remarks, we discussed the relationship between ordinary and extraordinary and whether this relationship is different, or similar, in the humanities and in law. The ideas and themes of that conversation inspired me to write this book. I had already been focusing (and publishing) on exemplarity, singularity and generality for some years, but an image that emerged

 | DOI 10.1163/9789004381315_002

then and there, in New York, pushed me to undertake a larger enterprise. In this inspiring image, the singular, extraordinary instance stands in front of the general norm and calls it into question. By this act of interpellation, a void, or hole, appears at the core of the general norm.

Here, I am interested in the tension between the ordinary and the extraordinary: it is at that juncture where the content and the sense of normativity originate and are performed. Yet, it is because of the indeterminate nature of normativity that we cannot really define what it is and how it works and so we can only find samples of norms under different forms or labels: they can be positive and abstract, or they can be embodied in singular cases that acquire the force of norms. In both cases, the norm is an *empty space*. Extraordinary cases (that work as general norms but remain singular instances) can fill this empty space. Those cases, in turn, can mediate between different values and in particular between the values that are already part of the normative order and those that emerge from society. In other words, the whole idea of normativity is a necessary invention that we should not try to define but that we should instead try to *observe*. This book is an attempt to bridge the use and theory of normativity through a series of perspectives drawn from the fields of art and law. More precisely, it is an attempt to observe the dynamic between what is considered ordinary and what is considered extraordinary in these two fields. The argument underlying the theses I develop here could be summarized as follows: (1) laws are abstract and do not provide what Nancy Fraser calls "normative traction", that is, they seem incapable of doing so as they are formulated to direct our judgments and actions; (2) extraordinary cases provide us with paradigmatic situations of application (that is, they function as heuristic criteria of application) and of solution of conflicts through a new equilibrium of values and interests; (3) thus, extraordinary cases provide some mediation between competing values and suggest the possibility to recognize a different (new, and in some sense revolutionary) norm.

In order to proceed in this theoretical enterprise, I want to suggest a way of reading normativity both in art and law from the perspective of the singular artwork and jurisprudential case. Such a way of approaching normativity is familiar to the Western tradition of thought since the emergence of the first exemplary narratives, among which the life of Christ constitutes a paradigm of reference. Jesus Christ embodies a normativity that recognizes the order, but that shows a different interpretation of that order in relation to the values that are outside of it. I will thus start by making reference to the paradigmatic *exemplum*. The life of Jesus Christ, like his deeds and death, touches upon the relevant theoretical questions concerning the relationship between ordinary and extraordinary. As a matter of fact, the present, living testimony of Jesus and his repetition of the sentence "but I say unto you" recall the distinctive force of the embodied norm—which is different from that of the written norm. Jesus expresses the distinction between the positive, written and general norm, on the one side, and the contingency of the singular life, on the other. In this opposition, on the one hand we find the norm of the Torah, general and abstract, valid for all men, with its infinite validity; on the other hand, in a parallel and not necessarily alternative system ("but" indicates the coexistence of the two levels of normativity), there is his voice: contingent, human, finite, mortal. This opposition also reflects the distinction between the textual and the oral tradition of normativity. It seems that at least five times in the *New Testament* Jesus utters the following sentence: "but I say unto you". In opposition to what had been said "by them of old time", Jesus distinguishes his voice through the sentence "but I say unto you". As anticipated, we are in front of a double normative code. On the one hand, we find what has already been said by the old wise men of old time, in other words what has been accepted and conventionally recognized as a norm: the ordinary. On the other hand, we find what does not yet have the legitimation of a norm and is being presented as something that could have the force of a norm but has a different form. In other words, we are in front of the extraordinary. The voice of Jesus is heard and must be considered valid (this is what he claims) because he has an authority and because of its authenticity. The scribes, on the contrary, have written something that certainly has a validity but whose authority can be undermined by that of the living and embodied norm (Jesus). When the embodied norm (the extraordinary) first encounters the written norm (the ordinary), the limits of both codes emerge. One is static, the other dangerously human. The witnesses of this encounter are astonished at the new norm who performs his normative force.

To repeat: on the one hand we find the written norm, taken for granted, legitimized by tradition, history, time, iteration. A norm based on the authority of the scribes who have "posed" it (the law of Moses). On the other hand, we find the embodied, living norm (Jesus and his word): this is a new voice, a contingent existence that claims to be capable of adding something to the content of the norm written by the scribes. There have been different interpretations of this relationship: according to some, the expression "but I say unto you" indicates a collision between the law of Moses and the embodied norm, and it thus refers to a concrete contrast between written and embodied normativity. It seems, instead, that Jesus does not want to destroy the law of the scribes: rather than contradicting the teaching of the law, the Sermon on the Mount explained and applied this teaching as it had never been done before. The extraordinary life shows the limits of the pre-existing normative order and yet, at the same time, it validates it. Jesus applies the teaching of the

Torah, emphasizing the full spirit of the law. He recognizes the importance and the authority of the written norm of Moses, but he suggests it is read, interpreted, and applied differently for various reasons. As stated before, the example of Christ contains some of the most relevant theoretical issues that I will be discussing in this work: (i) the tension between ordinary and extraordinary that characterizes the (empty) space of normativity is mirrored in the dialectic between Jesus' words and the words of the Old Testament; (ii) Jesus' words are extraordinary insofar as they are uttered by the son of God, but also because of their comparatively revolutionary content and because they are perceived as extraordinary in a specific context and by the *sensus communis* of the time; (iii) their being extraordinary gives them normative force.

This work concerns the opposition between the ordinary, that is, what is known and categorized and can be related to a certain order, and the extraordinary, which on the contrary is unexpected and does not fall into a defined category. I examine how this opposition works, respectively, in art and in law. More specifically, the phenomena considered in this book are of the following type:

(a) *In art*: I will consider the emergence of a particular artwork as exemplary within the field of art. Just like in the legal field, the field of art has its rules, its criteria. When an artwork breaks the precedent established norms and becomes itself a model, like in the case of Warhol's *Brillo Box* (1964), I will look into how a new genre can be produced through the singularity of the exemplary artwork.

(b) *In law*: I will consider the emergence of a particular case as an exemplary standard of reference in jurisprudential interpretation such as for instance *Brown v. Board of Education* (1954) or *United States v. Jones* (2012). The singular case, both in common law and in civil law systems, is the extraordinary that calls into question the general norm. The extraordinary in law is the singularity that questions the general norm by posing a specific question and by showing its limits.

Positioned at the intersection of the disciplinary discourses of art and law, this book's argument is grounded on the following assumptions.

(i) Normativity is an edge, an empty space between ordinary and extraordinary and a line both of separation and of contact between an order and what is outside of this order. Normativity identifies a space that at the same time separates but also puts in contact that which is inside and outside the dominant order. Without the interpellation of the extraordinary to the order of norms, it would be unnecessary to imagine the order and the normative force of the general norms. So this is a work about the fundamental function of the singularity both in art and law.

(ii) The relationship between ordinary and extraordinary is complex: it works in more than one direction and serves different functions. The singular artwork or case that emerges as extraordinary invites us to reflect on the rhetorical force of the singularity (which constitutes an argument to validate a certain reasoning), on the logic involved in it (inductive, and not deductive), on its didactic and normative force (rooted in ancient exemplarity), and on its epistemic function. Extraordinary singularities bring into existence new artistic genres and new jurisprudential trends. This means that the extraordinary artwork and the extraordinary jurisprudential decision convey a form of knowledge and interpretation of the artistic and of the juridical world.

The specific rhetorical force of the extraordinary case is that of the Latin *exemplum*, which intersects with its didactic and normative function. In order for a singular artwork or jurisprudential case to be considered extraordinary, it needs to be perceived as such within a context and thus the specific rhetorical force of the *exemplum* entails a reflection on the role played by the *sensus communis* in the process of "promotion" of the singularity into an extraordinary case that can create a new genre or a new jurisprudential trend, i.e. that can work as a model for further cases.

(iii) The logic of the extraordinary singularity is opposed to the type of reasoning that goes from general to particular. The extraordinary calls into question the ordinary, like in the cases considered in this book, that is to say Warhol's works—as examples of extraordinary singularities in art—and jurisprudential cases like *Brown* or *Obergefell*, that is to say cases that produce revolutions in legal interpretation.

(iv) The extraordinary case becomes a model for further cases and, through its exemplary force, it can be used to illustrate how something should be: it has didactic force. Like in Rousseau's *Emile*, the extraordinary individuality is such because it (or he or she) is not like anyone else: Emile is like every other man and, yet, he is not like every other man. He is typically exemplary: he remains human and, at the same time, he functions as a model.

(v) The extraordinary case has a very specific force—as a consequence of its normative value. And yet, it maintains the characteristics of the individual narrative or event. It is a means for conveying information and knowledge through individual events, conflicts, facts, stories and not through generalizations.

More generally, and in relation to all these assumptions, we could say that the extraordinary case is thus an expression of the artistic and juridical culture and proves, as Warburg or Cassirer would say, that human beings are most fundamentally *symbolic* animals interposing systems of signs or systems of expression between themselves and the world. The extraordinary singularity—both in art and the law—incorporates an expressive function, a representative function, and a semantic function: all of these functions intersect with one another. Following Cassirer,[1] we could distinguish the functions of the extraordinary singularity accordingly. More specifically, we could say that the most basic and primitive type of symbolic meaning is *expressive* meaning, which derives from what Cassirer calls the expressive function (*Ausdrucksfunktion*)—which is concerned with the experience of events in the world around us as charged with affective significance (desirable or hateful, comforting or threatening). The *cas extraordinaire* plays a crucial function also for what concerns the epistemic level, since it is supposed to convey also a truth-content: the singularity can have a symbolic meaning and this concerns its *significative* function (*Bedeutungsfunktion*). The representative function (*Darstellungsfunktion*) of the case is a consequence of the other functions: since it has the capacity to express and to signify beyond itself, the extraordinary singularity is capable of representing other entities. For instance, the exemplary jurisprudential decisions used for impact litigations (see *Part* 2) in the United States are chosen and used as symbols or allegories of the rights revolutions. They represent desires and needs of many people, much beyond the two or more parts that participate in the singular litigation.

As also argued in *Language and Myth*,[2] the extraordinary case illustrates *more* than the general and abstract norm, since it provides an image containing singular names, times and stories that are easy to recognize. The singular artwork or the singular jurisprudential case bring with them their relation with the factuality and with the course of events, in other words with the way things happen or have happened. Thus, as singular images, they have both an independent content and an immanent meaning. The case contains a *myth* (the individual narrative, like the story of Linda Brown in *Brown v. Board of Education*) which, for its extraordinary character, is interconnected with the *historìa*. In the Aristotelian tradition, the narrative (*mythos*) can be more universal than the series of events, of history (*historìa*), since the singular narrative describes events that are necessary and yet have a normative force, while *historìa* is limited to particular and contingent facts.

1 Cassirer (1923, 1925a).
2 Cassirer (1925b).

In the *Force of the Example*, Alessandro Ferrara refers to Max Weber when trying to explain why, behind the exemplarity of the singularity, there is always a selective process:

> any object, whether natural or cultural, contains many more constitutive elements than the number we can possibly be able to investigate during our finite lives. It is our finitude that enjoins us to adopt a perspective and to select the elements worth knowing more closely from the exorbitant number of knowable aspects, lest we end up knowing nothing. A map of a continent as large as the continent itself, which leaves out nothing, is totally useless. Now the point is that such selection of what is worth knowing and what we need not bother to know is an act that cannot be justified solely along cognitive lines, in terms of an *adaequatio intellectuset rei*, which obviously cannot have taken place yet. On the contrary, only on the basis of the hermeneutic foreunderstanding concerning the "worth-knowingness" of the object of knowledge—a foreunderstanding of which we need not be aware—can we speak of truth in a non subjectivistic sense.
>
> FERRARA 2008, 6

The emergence of a specific case as extraordinary is thus crucial and oscillates between a pure realist "emergence" of the singularity and an intentional selection and validation through the *sensus communis* in the Kantian sense. This double dynamic allows for a re-signification of the singularity in terms of a universal model (a sort of "universal singularity") thanks to its mediation between form and content, and between reality and thought: the singularity is the space in between the ordinary and the extraordinary. In this space, the rhetorical and epistemic forces of the norm interact.

Part 1: The Extraordinary in Art

1 *The Extraordinary and the Exceptional*

There would be no extraordinary case without an idea of "order": a case is extraordinary since it creates an issue with an established, conventional order. It poses a question and challenges the limits of the norm. The ordinary is the expected, what corresponds to an existing definition and that belongs to an *ordo*, to a certain order of things. Ordinary is thus what conforms to the dominant order. In other words, it is what we call customary, regular, and usual. Extraordinary is what instead is out of the dominant order. The extraordinary is not like the exceptional. The exceptional is the product of an exclusion (*exceptio*, from *excipere*—to take out). The process of exclusion entails the validity of an existing system of rules: *exceptio probat regulam in casibus non exceptis*, in other words the exceptional case illustrates the validity of the rule for all the situations which are not exceptional—thus for the situations that follow a general rule. Unlike the exceptional, the extraordinary is not just what is excluded from the realm of the ordinary: rather, it is what calls into question the ordinary and indicates a potential new interpretation of a general order. Unlike the exception, the extraordinary case does not confirm the norm but it calls it into question by indicating the possibility a different norm. The extraordinary is what proves that a different order might have its own validity: it does not prove the validity of the rule; on the contrary, it proves that a different order might be possible. The extraordinary singularity reflects a critical attitude, or denaturalization, or making strange, similar to that described by Foucault.[3] The extraordinary, unlike the exceptional, challenges the general assumption and indicates the necessity of its reformulation. It is the space of transformation or of reformulation of the norm.

Let us consider the case of Warhol's *Brillo Box*, an artwork which has attracted philosophers' interest since its creation.[4] Duchamp's ready-mades were already extraordinary and had already illustrated the necessity of defining again the distinction between an ordinary object used in daily life and an artwork. With (and since) *Brillo Box*, the category of the artworks included also ordinary objects used in daily life. Though Duchamp's works were already extraordinary and revolutionary, Warhol's works contributed to establish the ready-made as a category within the broader category of the artistic object. With this work, Warhol questioned the dominant definition of art, and thus the normative order grounding such a conceptual framework. Andina writes that "*Brillo Box* is an object with a background, one of great philosophical interest, which lies behind the story of the art work".[5] It is a small masterpiece, and much more. Its history is made up of different stories. It is an artwork, but before that it was the creation of a designer working in advertising, whose aim was to show that *Brillo pads* were an effective cleaning tool for the kitchen. An ordinary object (though possibly aesthetically interesting) is transformed into an extraordinary artistic object, into something that is not grouped together with similar objects from the past according to prior criteria regulating artistic

3 See specifically Foucault (1988, 152–156).

4 See as main literature Arthur Danto (1992); for a very good discussion about Danto's arguments also in relation to law, see Tiziana Andina (2017, 2018).

5 Andina (2017, 14).

categorization. Actually, Warhol's *Brillo Box* is not an ordinary object in a literal sense; Warhol created objects that looked like a Brillo Box through printing techniques. They are screen prints. Unlike the *Mona Lisa*, which is an exceptionally beautiful work of art whose originality did not problematize its inclusion within the category of paintings, *Brillo Box* challenges order and regularity in artistic demarcation and categorization, by calling into question the norms regulating the definition of art.

Brillo Box is extraordinary because it is an object known to everyone, a companion of the daily life of many Americans. Its extraordinary value is not given by some exterior characteristic, but by how it is made, by where it is displayed—in an art gallery—and by whom it is produced—a renowned artist. The object is not extraordinary in itself, but there are a number of elements that contribute in making it possible for it to stand out of the established order. Among these aspects, the commitment of the artist certainly plays a crucial role. Duchamp and Warhol wanted to break an established rule: the extraordinary character of the object is not given by the object itself, but it is a consequence of the commitment of the artist, who wants to prove the possibility of existence of a different normativity. An object is valued as extraordinary first of all by its author. This makes it the case for a box containing cleaning pads to be considered as a valuable artistic object. What is specifically interesting from the point of view of the present essay is the revolutionary force of *Brillo Box*.

Those who first saw *Brillo Box* in an art gallery were challenged because the nature of the object was, indeed, undoubtedly revolutionary: in front of them, they found a series of items perceptually indistinguishable from scrubbing-pad boxes that they could find in a supermarket. The traditional criteria for categorizing an object as an artistic object were challenged and, with them, the whole definition of art. *Brillo Box* is the perfect example of what an extraordinary case can do in a field, like art, governed by an order of norms (though less formalized than juridical norms).

In front of the unknown, every normative system has two choices: its exclusion and its inclusion. Excluding corresponds to recognizing the exceptional nature of the singularity, which is considered as a single occurrence and does not challenge the validity of the existing categorization. Including the unknown, or what appears to indicate the necessity to rephrase the norm, means to reconsider the content of the norm. In both cases, the general and abstract idea of the work of art is challenged, because the new object can either be treated as a revolutionary work of a new artistic genre—and it can thus be considered as "extraordinary"—or it can be treated as an exception that confirms the validity of the established order of norms. Anyhow, the extraordinary in art calls into question the normative constraints of the definition of art.

A prior order of things is challenged by what is *extra-ordinem*. The extraordinary character of the singular case opposes the content of the norm that defines the nature of the artistic object. On what are the extraordinary aesthetic properties of a singular artwork based? For Kendall Walton, an artwork's aesthetic properties always depend on non-aesthetic properties, that is to say the fact that some properties are judged as specific aesthetic properties, and among these as extraordinary ones, is related to the appreciation.[6] Among these non-aesthetic properties, some are standard properties, some are variable. A property is standard when it is among those properties in virtue of which artworks in a specific category fall into that category. A property is instead considered variable if it is not related to the fact that an artwork belongs to a category: having or not having a property which is variable is irrelevant as far as categorization is concerned. Walton also distinguished counter-standard properties, that is to say those properties that would exclude an artwork from a category. Interesting and useful may it be, this distinction among properties of artworks is never entirely sufficient to classify them, and it is for this reason that often innovative, and in some sense "revolutionary" objects can call into question the categorization of artistic works. In the process of categorization, beyond the function played by properties and by appreciation, a crucial role is played by the intention of the author.

Walton outlines diverse causes of our perceiving artworks in certain categories of art and thus diverse reasons for distinguishing between what is ordinary (and belongs undoubtedly to a category) and what is extraordinary. Often, our appreciation of an artwork is influenced by other works we are familiar with: the more works of a similar sort we have experienced, the more likely it is that we perceive a singular object within that category, because we have more familiarity with the standard and variable properties of a certain category (form of art, or genre).

An important role can be played by art critics as well: if we have heard other people say something about works we are experiencing, their judgement can influence our appreciation and thus the value acquired by the singular artwork. In some sense, the way we are introduced to the particular artwork can influence our appreciation. Walton writes:

> If a Cezanne painting is exhibited in a collection of French Impressionist works, or if before seeing it we are told that it is French Impressionist, we are more likely to see it as French Impressionist than if it is exhibited in

6 Walton (1970).

> a random collection and we are not told anything about it beforehand. I will say that a feature of a work is standard for a particular person on a particular occasion when, and only when, it is standard relative to some category in which he perceives it, and is not contra standard relative to any category in which he perceives it.
>
> WALTON 1970, 342

Judgment about the ordinary or extraordinary character of a singular artwork (and, similarly, of a singular jurisprudential case) is thus based on different criteria of categorization, among which the comparison with precedent, similar singularities also plays an important role. Moreover, the norms of production of the artwork can also be considered as criteria of categorization and appreciation.

The categorization of art as discussed by Walton entails that if a work differs too significantly from the standard properties of a category, or from the norms of production, we might not perceive it in that category and thus that work can indicate a different system of norms, that is to say the possibility of categorizing it differently.[7] So, a sculpture which constantly moves would be radically different from traditional sculptures. All the same, a small colored corner in an entirely black and white picture would be disconcerting. Should it be considered an exceptional version of black and white pictures? Or an extraordinary case of colored (for just that tiny little corner) picture? Or should there be a third option between these two?

Conclusively, and in relation to the themes and questions of the present book, we could say that how a work affects us aesthetically, what properties it seems to have and what properties we are inclined to see in it—depend on which properties are considered standard, which variable, and which could appear as counter-standard. Thus, appreciation depends on criteria that precede the contingent moment in which we enter in contact with the singular object. Something is extraordinary, or ordinary, also according to these standard and variable properties, and not just because it is valued as extraordinary in a contingent situation.

2 *The Mediocre*

The extraordinary character of the revolutionary artistic object challenges the distinction between originality and mediocrity: if we follow Hegel, art should perform the oppositional movement of simultaneously differentiating itself

7 Walton (1970, 353).

from the everyday while being also part, at the same time, of the ordinary aspects of life, of what literary critique has termed the "middle" of life. As noted by Paul Fleming in the introduction to his book *Exemplarity and Mediocrity*:

> If there is one thing art cannot be and still be art, it is quotidian or common. From its cultic origins through the imperative of originality and up to the provocation of anti-art, art by definition differs from everyday life—whether by idealizing the world, distinguishing itself from craftsmanship, refusing to participate in the logic of exchange or, at its extreme, by so approximating the everyday that the question "is this art?" becomes the paradoxical mode of art's continuation.
>
> FLEMING 2009, 1

Interestingly, this oscillation between ordinary and extraordinary—or, in different terms, between mediocrity and exemplarity—characterizes, *mutatis mutandis*, also the structure of juridical normativity. A clarification about the term 'mediocrity' is necessary; I do not use it as an aesthetically value-laden term expressing an aesthetic judgment. With 'mediocre' I do not mean 'bad', but I refer to a type of object that is inspired by what is ordinary.

As I shall discuss in *Part 2* of the present work, the extraordinary character of the singular juridical case calling into question the general and abstract norm is characterized by the same dialectic: the peculiar character of the singular case stems precisely from its aspects of singularity and at the same time those are the aspects closer to life. The singular case is at the same time extraordinary—i.e., it exceeds the boundaries of the abstract norm—and ordinary in a different sense—i.e., it has aspects of ordinary life, of mediocrity, that distinguish it from the general and abstract norm. We shall thus see that also in legal discourse the exemplary case conveys a very specific normative force that is closer to reality and to everyday life.

Let us return on *Brillo Box*. This case shows that the difference between ordinary and extraordinary is subtle, contested and changeful. And in fact, as Fleming notes, the modern hero like Werther becomes a paradigm by embodying a series of average characteristics. He desires the ordinary: he does not desire something other than the order of the bourgeois man. He wants to feel recognized and to have his place in the middle class. He wants to be pigeonholed and to enter into a system. The exemplary modern hero thus shows the contradictory relationship between exceptionality and mediocrity. Goethe's hero becomes exemplary by desiring to be recognized as someone *like the all the others*. And because of this desire, he is considered original.

Mediocrity translates into a pulsion to feel recognized by the community where the individuals that count mostly live, and among them Lotte in particular. Though the order of social norms of the middle class is also very distant from Werther's impulses, desires and process of individuation, he cannot feel content until he can feel included in that order. This tension characterizes the relationship between ordinary and extraordinary, or between mediocrity and exemplarity, continuously. *Die Leiden des jungen Werther* (1774) manifests this tension in a paradigmatic way: the genius is permanently confronted with an attraction for the (sometimes trivial) aspects of everyday life. The opposition between extraordinary and ordinary is particularly evident in the case of Werther because he embodies the perfect example of an extraordinary young man—an intelligent, sensitive member of the educated middle class in Germany, an artist—and yet he is attracted by the ordinary life of middle class individuals. He straddles two worlds: the extraordinary life of the artist and the normal bourgeois life made of meetings and frivolous conversations. Though from the perspective of the extraordinary subject, that is to say the artist, Werther recognizes that the prosaic reality of the bourgeois life has nothing to offer art; yet, he wants to be recognized by the members of the middle class. All the norms governing the life of the middle class (rules of conduct, an economy of restraint, the importance of usefulness) are in a relationship of contradiction with artistic production. Middle class generates measure in every aspect of life, while the artist would know no limit: the genius aspires to offer a different, revolutionary idea of measure. The ideal nature of the artist is to neglect all restriction and to propose an alternative measure: therefore, the task of the young artist (Werther) should not be to become a perfect bourgeois gentleman but, instead, to reject every notion of measure, as well as of conformity to customs and to rules. The natural instinct of the artist would normally be to take leave of the established rules of the bourgeois life in order to live, exactly, the life of an artist. Paul Fleming notes how Werther even decides to follow the canons of genial art and this to take leave also from the norms of aesthetics. The two opposing codes, the ordinary life of the middle class man and the extraordinary life of the artist, are not compatible: if the ordinary man moderates all his capacities—for what concerns love, choices, energy, resources—the artist would never moderate or ration them.

Against this background, one would be tempted to say that art and everyday life, in the case of Werther, would never encounter each other. However, it is quite the opposite, since the genius is attracted by everyday life: as a matter of fact, Werther does not fall in love with an artist or with someone who is attracted by extremes, but with unexceptional gestures that belong to every domestic realm. The attraction of the extraordinary (Werther) towards the ordinary (Lotte and her world) reflects the attraction between the extraordinary singularity—both in art and law—and the normative order called in question by the singular case. The more the mediocrity of Lotte emerges, the more Werther falls in love and is attracted by her: when she confesses that her favorite authors in literature are those who allow her to see her world represented, and that describe things very similar to those happening to her, Werther is completely captured. Paul Fleming depicts this contradiction in details: Werther struggles to conceal his emotions about what Lotte says, even though this might look weird, since what she says is absolutely banal and distant from his language, from his taste and from his world. Charlotte's criteria for judging good literature are entirely prosaic and reflect the typical desires of the middle class: the identification with a familiar environment, the recognition of those situations that resemble one's own life, the high value placed on domestic life, which constitutes the foundation for all conception of the world. In the aforementioned scene where Lotte tells Werther about her taste, her desires appear in all their limitedness, since they only aim at reproducing the existing order of things: on the opposite, Werther's desire knows no limit. Fleming writes:

> But this is the point of the novel viewed from the tension between exemplarity and mediocrity: the original art of the genius is to transfigure mediocrity, just as Werther's desire transfigures the bourgeois life that runs counter to art. Although Werther, in his unbridled and uncontainable passion, assumes a position opposite bourgeois life, what he ultimately desires is to take the bourgeois Albert's place. Werther doesn't desire something other than the bourgeois order; he wants his place in it, at Lotte's side.
>
> FLEMING 2009, 6

Werther's desire to be pigeonholed and to enter into the bourgeois system is stronger than his artistic genius. He wants to enter into a system, as if the fact of being part of the system could save him from his sufferings. The way the desire emerges—its strength, its extraordinary and excessive nature—is different from the very content of that desire, which speaks about a will of recognition and which is utterly common. The extraordinary individual, Werther, is thus very ambiguous: he succeeds as a genial lover (at least for what concerns his feelings), but he fails as an artist. He cannot be extraordinary in every aspect of his life: he loves like an artist, but his art is mediocre. Even the way he judges his own work reflects his contradictory and ambiguous nature both as an artist and as a lover: he assesses his own work as "well organized" and "interesting", which are typical expressions of the bourgeois code. His artistic aspiration is extraordinary, but his production is ordinary, to the point of being mediocre. Werther aims to be a genius; but the idea of genius should reflect impossibility of repetition, uniqueness, distance from mass production. What he finally experiences is the fact of not being blessed by genius but, at least, to love in an extraordinary way. The singular, extraordinary individual thus carries a sort of attraction-distance for and from the average.

This digression into the extraordinary in Goethe recalls another important aspect of the relationship between ordinary and extraordinary, that is to say mimesis or imitation, which plays a crucial role both in art theory as well as in legal theory. In regulating forms of expression (art) and forms of life (law), and in establishing whether they fall or not within categories that have a normative force, both artistic and legal discourse have been characterized by processes of imitation (mimesis) of already existing models. Periods characterized by mimesis of existing models alternated to periods of innovation—i.e., avant-garde movements in art or fights for civil rights in law—which reversed the precedent genres and trends. As I argue in the section devoted to genre classification between ordinary and extraordinary,[8] genre classification in art resembles the emergence of jurisprudential trends in law: it is hard to explain the rules of this emergence, and in fact it is hard to define if there are any rules for the definition of these genres/trends. Yet it is undoubtable that there are trends in the various fields of juridical practice. For instance, there are specific tendencies in criminal law that change in time according to the political orientations and of the societal evolutions. Trends, just like genres in art, are often oriented by the rulings of the higher Courts—for instance, in the United States by rulings of the Supreme Court and in Italy by rulings of the Corte di Cassazione. There are obvious differences between the two systems: first and foremost, art does not have formal procedures for the recognition of hierarchies of sources of normativity and there are no higher or lower courts and institutions within the artistic realm and discourse. While there are interesting analogies between the two worlds, it is thus important to recognize the disanalogies between them in order to treat them properly.

Let us return to the field of art. On the one hand, in art history, there have been historical trajectories in which stylistic trends have become the canons, thus implicitly offering *standards of imitation* and *criteria of classification* for artworks. In the periods characterized by a tendency to reproduce by imitating, original art is considered extraordinary and even exemplary if it follows the rules of the models of artistic production—of the canons, in other

8 § 3.

words. In those phases, an artistic object is considered extraordinary if it has been realized by respecting the rules so well, that that object can be defined an "exemplary artwork". Here, the term 'exemplary' stands for "very good" or "very well executed" and not for "groundbreaking" or "revolutionary". In those phases, original art is exemplary when it corresponds to an accepted and pre-existing model of judgement. In other words, periods of art history can be distinguished broadly into two varieties: normal periods, where exemplarity is in perfect compliance with the norms, and revolutionary moments where exemplarity corresponds to the rejection of those norms. The extraordinary singularity does not have the same value at any time: at times it confirms a regularity in an exceptional way, while at other times it overturns the established regularity by proposing a new pattern.

It is likewise undoubtable, on the other hand, that there are periods in which 'original' and 'extraordinary' are terms used to indicate works that create a rupture with a tradition of precedent works: here, the extraordinary and exemplary singularity is instead what is out of the ordinary and embodies a revolutionary force. In both cases, the normative discourse (be it art or law) is connected to the understanding of the concept of "ordinary" and of "extraordinary" within a specific historical context. The break between the ancient and the modern understanding of what is "extraordinary" can be summarized as follows: whereas art in the wake of Aristotle's and Horace's respective *Poetics* is conceived as a series of rules and *exempla* to be followed (that is to say: exemplarity served as the basis for artistic production and the maintenance of tradition), modern art is defined by its originality. In modernity, exemplarity corresponds to original, groundbreaking and extraordinary art. Likewise, the treatment of the "genius", a typical embodied extraordinary singularity, reflects this variable understanding of the unique character of the singular case, life, or form of expression. We could refer to these different ways of being extraordinary as the *regular* extraordinary case—typical of antiquity, where the mimesis of models considered perfect is regarded as out of the ordinary—and the *revolutionary* extraordinary case—typical of modernity, where the capacity to establish a different regularity, and to be groundbreaking and innovative, is considered out of the ordinary.

As a matter of fact, in art theory another central *topos* is the figure of the belated genius, who came too early and was "too original": in order to be appreciated as such, the extraordinary singularity must somewhat connect in a timely fashion to dominant and yet contextually contingent criteria of artistic demarcation. The *sensus communis* changes, and the dominant values as well. Extraordinary and exemplary art often awaits an adequate reception. On the contrary, average art tends to fit comfortably into the art scene where it emerges.

Kant has noticed that unlike classical art, modern art values "exemplary originality", which the genius is capable of bringing to life: thus art's ideal is opposed to the ordinary, unexceptional, common, prosaic, and average. If, on the one hand, the originality of the genius is very important, on the other hand—as demonstrated by Paul Fleming reflections on mediocrity—modernity is also a turning point towards the average life. Thus, if on the one hand Werther is a genius and is like nobody else, he values the ordinary life of Lotte and her world and he wants—and needs—to feel recognized by that system of regularities which is the *bourgeoisie*.

2.1 Golden Mean(s), Old and New

The relationship between ordinary and extraordinary in art has gone through different phases, and has been characterized by at least two different ways of being extraordinary: on the one hand, the *regular* extraordinary case; on the other hand, the *revolutionary* extraordinary case. As it is well known, Horace's notion of the golden mean is derived from Aristotle's *Nicomachean Ethics*: according to his opinion, Aristotle's ethical apparatus is based on the idea that the extremes (i.e. what is out of the ordinary) must be balanced and contained. The average, even mediocrity, can preserve the *aretè*, which translates a type of virtue that can lead to excellence. In this period, the ordinary is the extraordinary. The whole idea of the good life, in fact, is built around an aesthetic judgement of balance and measure: extremes must be avoided. The *regular* extraordinary case is the mean (though a "golden", particular, kind of mean). Interestingly, in order to explain the value of averageness, Horace refers to the lawyer and to the artist. In many areas of human life (such as, for instance, law and art), mediocrity has its value and is synonym of balance and equilibrium. However, there is a clear difference between law and art: the mediocre lawyer is actually valuable, the mediocre poet, or sculptor, is not.

Yet, the exceptional capacities of the artist, in antiquity, must not reflect the desire to break the rules or the canons of beauty: the excellent and extraordinary artwork must reflect the criteria of beauty fixed by the standards or exemplary models of beauty. The artist is required to observe the conventional genres and subject matters. As aforementioned, with modernity there is a sharp shift of paradigm. In particular with Kantian aesthetics, the goal is no longer to follow canons and *exempla* through imitation, but through originality: it is only the extraordinary singularity, the *revolutionary extraordinary*, the very original instance, that has the capacity to establish new—and exemplary—modes of art production. The notion of mediocrity thus undergoes a profound change, a reversal, in which Kant's aesthetics plays a crucial role, in particular for what concerns the idea of the genius: the genius is by definition the individual that embodies a state of exception, that goes beyond the ordinary and that questions a dominant idea of "normality" and "regularity". The genius knows no authorizing procedures because its extraordinary character is exactly what gives it authority. The notion of reflective judgement recognizes that there can be no objective rules for taste, and that the singularity is the only measure of uniqueness. The genius does not imitate; on the contrary, he builds a new style and becomes himself a source of inspiration: the genius gives the rule.

When discussing the extraordinary character of the genius, Kant distinguishes two modes of aesthetic presentation: on the one hand, the manner (or "*modus aestheticus*")—which does not respect any measure and is self-justified by its unique character; on the other hand, the method or "*modus logicus*" which is based on certain principles that should be followed. The first corresponds to the *revolutionary* extraordinary case while the second to the *regular* extraordinary case. The relationship between the two *modi* has always been under redefinition and it is once again Paul Fleming that suggests a change of paradigm in the way the relationship between the ordinary, the extraordinary, and mediocrity is conceived in the contemporary:

> While the dilemma of exemplarity and mediocrity certainly doesn't end in the nineteenth century, it assumes a different form in the twentieth century for various reasons.
>
> FLEMING 2009, 163

First with the avantgarde, and then with the emergence of contemporary art, the processes of production, definition, and appreciation of art start challenging the boundaries of the traditional definition of the artistic object. This change is driven by the emergence of extraordinary singularities like Warhol's *Brillo Box*. If, before, the judgement about the definition of art was an aesthetic one, now it becomes and ontological problem: art is whatever is called art, or the artist thinks or wants to be art, or what the audience or the market accepts *as* art. The typical examples of this new shift in the relationship between ordinary and extraordinary are the ready-mades: as already discussed above, for instance, the works by Duchamp or Andy Warhol. In the XX century, the distinction between art and non-art does not concern a judgment about the extraordinary beauty of some object, nor the content of the work of art: the criteria of classification change completely.

2.2 The Force of the Singularity (in Art and Law)

The singularity (i.e., the singular jurisprudential decision, the singular story, the singular artwork) has a specific force which is rooted in its uniqueness and—most importantly—in its familiarity and closeness to the ordinary. The extraordinary is always, by definition and necessarily, a singularity. And yet, it is a specific type of singularity, i.e., that type that acquires—for contextual reasons—the force of a norm. In *The Force of the Example*, Alessandro Ferrara writes:

> The dichotomic view of our world as split between facts and values, facts and norms, *Sein* and *Sollen*, *is* and *ought*, descriptive and normative accounts has misled us into overlooking the specific relevance and force of exemplars: namely, of entities, material or symbolic, that are as they should be, atoms of reconciliation where *is* and *ought* merge and, in so doing, liberate an energy that sparks our imagination. The "thirdness" of the *force of examples* with respect to the force of facts or things (usually investigated by the empirical sciences) and that of ideas or of the *ought* (which remains the domain of practical philosophy) has combined its peripheralizing effect with the fact that the most articulate account of it has been couched by Kant in terms of an inquiry into the beautiful, thereby suggesting that exemplarity and its force belong in a special domain of our philosophical world: aesthetics.
>
> FERRARA 2008, X, *Preface*

The singularity has a force that exerts appeal on us in all realms of life: artistic, political, religious, legal, economic, social, medical, and industrial. This quality of bridging reality and normativity, facts and norms has been called in different ways: authenticity, beauty, perfection, charisma, aura.

One should notice that each historical context attributes a different relevance to the singularity. Ferrara writes:

> Political traditions and philosophical conceptions differ on the extent to which they allow the force of the example, and judgment, to play a role within their framework [...].
>
> FERRARA 2008, 99

The singularity has this force for some reason which is not easy to define a priori and once for all. As discussed above, in different periods of history a case emerges as an extraordinary singularity if it respects the rules so perfectly that is not like the other cases (*regular* extraordinary case) or if it breaks the rules so clearly to establish a new regularity (*revolutionary* extraordinary case). In both cases, the details of the case contribute in making it extraordinary because they are what distinguish that extraordinary singularity from the mass of other ordinary singularities. Let us take, for instance, two jurisprudential decisions that certainly fall within the category of *revolutionary* extraordinary cases: *Brown v. Board of Education* and *Obergefell v. Hodges*, both decided by the American Supreme Court.

Let us begin with the most recent case, *Obergefell v. Hodges* (2015), which immediately became a landmark civil rights case: in it, the Supreme Court of the United States ruled that the right to marry should be guaranteed to same-sex couples by both Due Process Clause and Equal Protection Clause of the Fourteenth Amendment to the United States Constitution. The ruling was particularly revolutionary because, for the first time, in all fifty states it became mandatory to perform and recognize the marriages of same-sex couples, on the very same terms as the marriages of opposite-sex couples, including all the accompanying rights and responsibilities. The comment of Barack Obama became a slogan at that time: he started the press conference saying "love is love", meaning that the time for differentiating between better or worse love relationships was over. The singular extraordinary case became an index to refer to equal marriage rights across the whole territory of the United States of America (and also at a global level). Obama declared the singular character of the ruling, defining it first of all a victory for Jim Obergefell and the other plaintiffs in the case. But the case was at the same time, and this was extraordinary, a victory for all the gay and lesbian couples who had been fighting until then for their fundamental civil rights. Moreover, Obama defined it a victory for their children, for all the friends and allies who had supported those couples in their fights, hoping together that things could change. At a more general level, he claimed that *Obergefell* should be considered a victory for America and for equality: everyone, after *that* singular decision, would become more free. Obama defined Jim Obergefell the "protagonist" of this fight: his individual story, from the moment of that decision, was no longer an individual series of events but it had become a *mythos*, a universal singularity.

Though often in law changes and progresses come in small increments, by making some steps further and some steps back, *Obergefell* demonstrated that sometimes justice arrives like a thunderbolt in the orderly organized normativity of law and has the force to produce a revolution. Obama declared:[9] "What an extraordinary achievement". "What a vindication of the belief that

9 https://www.theguardian.com/us-news/2015/jun/26/obama-gay-marriage-speech-victory-for-america.

ordinary people can do extraordinary things. What a reminder of what Bobby Kennedy once said about how small actions can be like pebbles being thrown into a still lake, and ripples of hope cascade outwards and change the world." The extraordinary character of the singular case was extended to all similar cases by becoming a norm, a model for millions of other Americans who were (and are) still facing legal discriminations simply for who they are, for what they do or for who they love.

The story began when an Ohio man sued the state to get his name listed on his husband's death certificate; it went through years of campaigning by LGBT rights activists, important attorneys and many other couples waiting decades before getting to a ruling. From that story in Ohio, the case became an allegory of liberty in America: the petitioners were trying to reach that liberty by marrying someone of the same sex and by having their marriages considered lawful under the same conditions as marriages between persons of the opposite sex. At the end of the path which had started with the experience of one man in Ohio, there were scenes of jubilation all over the United States, and people belonging to very different realms—activists, politicians, and everyday people—hailing a victory of love and of equality. The judge whose vote was decisive, Justice Kennedy, wrote that "[the Supreme Court] cases have expressed constitutional principles of broader reach. In defining the right to marry these cases have identified essential attributes of that right based in history, tradition and other constitutional liberties inherent in this intimate bond".

With *Obergefell*, love and civil rights have won a fight: through the singular case, a general concept—love—and a broader fight, the fight for equality in marriage, were also affected. The singular story becomes an allegory of love and of civil rights. The scene outside the Supreme Court becomes part of the allegory, showing members of the Congress standing outside the Court together with human rights activitists and friends and family of Jim Obergefell. Among the crowd in Washington there was also Mark Takano, a gay member of the Congress who declared that the experience of being present at the scene was "profound and pointed", as he had the feeling that the Supreme Court had "thrown a huge wedding bouquet to LGBT people all across the country and couples are going to be rushing to catch that bouquet".[10] Even though legal obstacles were still present in the lives of homosexual individuals living in the United States (in relation to housing and employment discrimination, for instance), the barrier of marriage rights was abolished and that singular ruling—according to what Takano declared—had set the tone for new changes to come.

10 https://www.theguardian.com/us-news/2015/jun/26/obama-gay-marriage-speech-victory-for-america.

Other interviews with rights activists describe scenes of strong emotions: as soon as the news became public about the extraordinary ruling, men and women were in tears and overcome with emotion because the victory of Jim Obergell was also *their* victory: in this sense, the extraordinary case gained the universal force of a general and abstract norm. Through the singular case, law works on the lives of the people almost like literature: that is to say, it produces identification and reciprocal recognition. When we read *Madame Bovary*, we pay attention to the details of her daily life because it is *through* those details that we can identify with her world and it is *in* those details that our life and her life are somehow similar.

For Judge Kennedy, the right to marry—like all fundamental rights—does not come from ancient sources or from the past: fundamental rights need to be defined according to the spirit of the time, because they become real only when they are enacted and when they are interpreted by each person in her or his individual story. Thus, according to his view, rights are not static definitions: this extraordinary decision has shown that the order of rights and values, as established by positive laws, was called into question by the ruling in the case *Obergefell*.

Justice Roberts wrote one of the dissenting opinions in the case *Obergefell*. He wrote that the Supreme Court should not be a substitute of the legislative power: whether same-sex marriage should exist and whether it reflects correct values or not—should not be object of the judgement of the Court but of the legislative power. This is also the problem with extraordinary singularities: their revolutionary force can be considered also as a threat to a precedent equilibrium of powers. For Justice Roberts, under the Constitution Supreme Court judges have only the power to say what the law is, and not what it should be. The extraordinary singularity thus produces an earthquake also at the level of the distribution of powers: something similar happens in the realm of art, where the rules for categorization are usually established by authors, critics and other groups that have the authority to define them. The extraordinary case in art creates a problem with those definitions, and it does so by means of its presence.

The case also illustrates what the extraordinary singularity does to the abstract norm. The existing laws, before *Obergefell*, constituted a limit to the liberty of same-sex couples: they reflected a model of society were same-sex relationships were disapproved and this disapproval had translated into a long-lasting denial to same-sex couples of the right to marry. But the acceptance of the extraordinary case requires time. And, before the revolution was translated at the institutional level, months would pass: the uniform implementation of the new groundbreaking norm established by the extraordinary case needed to be integrated in the order—thus showing the constant oscillation between ordinary and extraordinary. Before the States implemented the new ruling, it took time: the extraordinary requires time to be accepted, understood, translated into the language of the authority. After *Obergefell*, the United States became the twenty-first state in the world to recognize marriage equality across the entire territory.

Years before this extraordinary case concerning marriage equality, *Brown v. Board of Education* (1954) had become the landmark ruling about desegregation: so, likewise, the history of civil rights in America had been affected by an extraordinary singularity.

The *mythos*, or series of events, could be summarized as follows: the father of Linda Brown had objected when she was not allowed to attend an all-white school in her neighborhood. The case got to the Supreme Court and came to symbolize one the most transformative and revolutionary proceedings in American history. Recently, Linda Brown died in Topeka and her death was narrated by the major newspapers all over the world.[11] The revolutionary force of *Brown v. Board of Education*, in all the articles reporting about the death of Linda Brown, emerged as a constitutive part of the life of this African American woman. Let us begin at the end of this extraordinary life that, because of its extraordinary character, became the paradigm of desegregation fights in America and all over the world.

Linda Brown was born on February 20th, 1943, in Topeka to Leola and Oliver Brown. Her (quite) ordinary story encountered the macrohistory of civil rights in the United States. It was a day in September 1950 and Linda's father, Oliver Brown, was taking her to the Sumner School. In an interview released to the press when she was already an adult, Linda tried to recall the feelings of that (extraordinary) day: she described a bright and sunny day, and she was walking briskly with her dad when they got to what appeared to Linda (who was a little child) as great steps. The steps of the school. The school rejected Linda: she could not be enrolled. Linda felt that something was going wrong, since her dad was becoming agitated: she could feel the tension being transferred from his hand to hers while they were walking back home. The school could deny Linda the enrollment according to the "separate, but equal" doctrine, which at that time was still in force. According to that doctrine, segregation in public offices and institutions was permitted.

Subsequently, Oliver Brown filed a suit against the Board of Education, and then the case (after the first levels of jurisdiction) got to the Supreme Court. In its ruling, the Supreme Court threw out the "separate, but equal" doctrine by declaring racial segregation illegal: it was not longer sufficient that students of

---

11 https://www.nytimes.com/2018/03/26/obituaries/linda-brown-symbol-of-landmark-desegregation-case-dies.html.

all races could afford equal facilities. They should be allowed to attend the same schools. According to the Supreme Court, the separation of African American children and of children belonging to other racial minorities was unjust: separating them from others of similar age solely because of their race was simply racist. Such separation had generated feelings of inferiority as to the status of the children excluded by the "all white" schools and that had meant a discrimination also within the community: this discrimination could affect their hearts and minds very deeply. By the time the Supreme Court got to the ruling, Linda Brown was attending an integrated high school; later, she became an educational consultant. She always remained, throughout the course of her life, the symbol of the fight for equal rights.

The name attached to the lawsuit, which ended with the extraordinary and revolutionary ruling, was Linda's father's, Oliver Brown. Yet the lawsuit that ended up in the United States Supreme Court represented also other families in other states. The consequences and ramifications of the ruling are still being felt and the name of Linda Brown is still used as a synonym of equal rights and of fights for equality.

But the extraordinary force of *Brown v. Board of Education* was not completely accidental, it seems. According to what Cheryl Brown Henderson, Linda's sister, recalls—an educational organization lobbying for civil rights had contacted Oliver Brown and had suggested him to find the nearest white school to their home, take his child and at least one witness, and try to enroll. Then, the members of this organization suggested Oliver to go back home and report to them and the press what he and his child had experienced. According to Cheryl Brown Henderson, in other words, *Brown v. Board of Education*, the most extraordinary and symbolic case of American jurisprudential history, was probably the result of a strategic litigation organized by an organization of civil rights activists, who needed singular extraordinary narratives to argue in favor of the abolition of segregation. As a matter of fact, Linda was interviewed many times during her adulthood and each time she reported the story of a quite serene childhood in a neighborhood which was quite integrated. She used to play with children that had Spanish-American origins, but also with children who were white, Indian and African-American. The school she was attending at the time of the famous episode on a September morning in 1943 was good and her family was not dissatisfied, despite the fact that it was a so called "black school"—following the "separate, but equal" doctrine. The only thing that seemed to create a real problem for Linda's father was actually the distance from home to get to school, since she had to walk through a rail yard and across a busy road, and then she had to take a bus (which, for a seven years old, was not ideal).

Brown and *Obergefell* show how the extraordinary singularity can create a new interpretive trend: after those two cases, marriage rights and the "separate, but equal doctrine" were treated differently.

Something similar happens in the artistic realm, where singular extraordinary artworks can bring into existence a new genre. In a recent essay about the function of particular details for exemplarity, it has been noted that an individual narrative emerges as exemplary within the literary field because of its extraordinary value.[12] What characterizes the process of exemplarity is that the case becomes exemplary by remaining particular, in other words it becomes extraordinary by remaining ordinary. Differently, if the case did not exhibit its particularity, we would be in front of a *facti species*, a *Tatbestand*. We would not be dealing with the process of exemplarity but with the process of subsumption, where the case is particular but, despite its particularity, it still belongs to a species and it falls into a model. In that process, instead of the particularity of the case, what counts is its mere particularity. This is the interpretation offered by György Lukács when discussing the subjectivity and the epiphany of the modernist narrative in light of the of allegory as examined by Walter Benjamin in *The Origin of the German Tragic Drama* (1963).

The approach of literary Modernism to the role and to the potential uses of the singularity is very different from the approach of literary Realism. For Modernism, every particularity can refer to something else, since the allegory plays a crucial function in the interpretation of the world and in the use of language. Subjectivity in Realism is, on the contrary, a central formal device for the description of the lives of those who are like everybody else. In this tension between ordinary and extraordinary, the selection of the relevant particulars (within the case) is a central process and this process is what creates a connection in the ordinary–extraordinary dichotomy and it is where the singular case emerges. In each context, the details can be treated differently, as proved by the literary experience. Modernism treats details as mere occasions, as allegories: they are not valued as such but only for their symbolic meaning. Realism emphasizes the importance of familiarity and even of the triviality of the particulars.

As underlined by Auerbach,[13] modernist literature tends to consider reality as a chance, as a passage of transition towards another dimension of meaning. In such a context, the particulars of the "bare life" acquire different meanings and values within different contexts: yet, it might sound like an exaggeration to claim that anything could be exemplary and that the judgement about the extraordinary character of a singularity depends strictly and only on the context.

---

12 Toracca (2018).

13 Mimesis (1946).

If we are not willing to accept an implausible absolute relativism on this type of judgement, we should thus focus on the appreciation of the case *as* an extraordinary instance *of something* specific. There must be a reason and a justification for the appreciation: such reason and justification lie in the features of the case, and specifically on those features that make it relevantly different from other—similar—cases (we could refer to these features in terms of its "thick" features). In a certain sense, and quite counter-intuitively, in order to be appreciated *as* extraordinary and thus as normative, the singularity must show its bareness, its nakedness, its proximity to the world of facts.

The theme of the extraordinary life and existence has also been at the center of the problem of individuation in the philosophy of life as elaborated by Jacques Derrida.[14] From the perspective of his philosophy of life, the interest for the singularity and for its specific characteristics can also be related to a traumatic experience. The case makes the contrast between lives and norms emerge: there are situations, experiences, and subjects that are in a position to testify in an exemplary way, to show a conflict or a problem or a contradiction. The singular life testifies to the effort to realize an individuation against or according to society, that is, against or according to an organized system of normativity. The singular life offers an image of the material relationship between a world of contingency and a world of necessity.

The singular life, as demonstrated by the paradigmatic and original life, the life of Jesus Christ, which is the archetype of the embodied norm, calls into question diverse levels of normativity (first of all: moral, juridical and regulative in a broader sense) because of its unique character. It is extraordinarily unique because it is defined by its aspects of particularity. When extraordinary, the individuality mediates between absolute particularity and absolute universality: the life of Christ is emblematic of this double code from which the force of the singularity originates. The ordinary individual life can show extraordinary characteristics and can thus acquire a normative value and force: the singularity can also justify a principle of "chosenness", like in the Jewish tradition.

According to the Torah, in order to justify the fact of having been chosen among other people, the singularity must be understood as individuality: which means, in its peculiarity and because of its original characteristics that distinguish it from other singularities. A specific treatment and a specific form of validity (and, in art and law, a specific normative force) are justified by the strong significance attributed to the aspects of particularity. For instance, in the case of *Brillo Box*, by the fact that those objects are: (i) aesthetically interesting

14 As broadly and deeply discussed in the work by Dana Hollander (2008). See also Irene Harvey (2002).

and even beautiful, as noted by Tiziana Andina; (ii) by the fact that they constitute a typical commonplace object. They are, in fact, not unusual objects that we only use or see in special occasions: they are truly ordinary, a common presence in one's everyday life. This is what attributes to them a specific "exemplarity", to follow Derrida: a term used to indicate the relationship between the transcendental and the factical, the singular and the universal.[15]

3 *Genre Classification*

The relationship between ordinary and extraordinary becomes crucial when facing the issue of defining a new artistic genre. For instance, as observed above, Warhol's *Brillo Box* or Duchamp's *Fountain* challenged the norms regulating the demarcation of the categories of art. By definition, the extraordinary case does not fall into a pre-defined and existing category and it is exactly for this reason that it is extraordinary. By questioning the nature and validity of the existing categories and genres, the extraordinary singularity, that is, the extraordinary artwork, like *Fountain*, does not only challenge a general idea of "order", but more specifically it questions the genre classification and its intrinsic normativity.

An artistic genre can be considered a principle of grouping similar works of art.[16] A genre is both a descriptive and a prescriptive notion; because of this double nature, a genre resembles a jurisprudential trend. That is to say, it resembles an established inclination to decide a certain type of case in a certain way. On the one hand, a genre can be used to group single elements as artworks of some kind, just like trends do something analogous with jurisprudential decisions; on the other hand, once it is accepted as a valid criterion of classification, a genre—as it happens with trends—acquires a normative force. For example, within the art form 'Literature' we group together works such as Dante's *Divine Comedy* and Flaubert's *Madame Bovary*, just as within the art form 'Music' we group together works such as Mozart's *Jupiter Symphony* and Cohen's *Take this Waltz*. Then, within those art forms, we distinguish different genres: for instance, novel and poetry within literature and classical and baroque music within music. In this sense, the artistic genre is a *descriptive* notion, a label that tells us something about a specific set of works of art. And yet, artistic genres seem to play not only a descriptive role but also a *normative* one. As claimed by Kendall Walton in *Categories of Art*,[17] categories affect our perception of artworks and thus their ontology is also influenced by pre-existing

15 Hollander (2008, 52).
16 Condello and Terrone (2017).
17 Walton (1970).

categories. On this, Enrico Terrone and I have recently engaged in a reflection which led us to claim that:

> We exploit genres not only in order to classify works of art but also in order to evaluate them. That is because we do not normally assess a work of art as such, but rather as belonging to a certain genre. For example, we can assess the *Mona Lisa* as a painting, i.e., with respect to certain expectations and standards that constitute the painting as an artistic genre. Likewise, we normally say "I read a wonderful novel," "I watched a terrible movie," or "I really liked that ballet," thereby suggesting that we experienced a work that was wonderful *as a novel*, or terrible *as a movie*, or really pleasurable *as a ballet*. In this sense genres play an essential role in the functioning of art, inasmuch as art is made for users and users enjoy works of art through the mediation of genres. As pointed out by Judith Jarvis Thomson, most (if not all) normative judgments rely upon a category that provides a standard of assessment for judgments about objects of that category. We do not normally assess an object only as the particular object. Rather, we assess an object by considering it as a member of a certain category, and this category provides us with a standard of assessment that allows us to formulate the judgment about that particular object.
>
> CONDELLO and TERRONE 2017, 39

The problem has been widely discussed also in literary theory: if *Don Quixote* is a Novel, is *Le Rouge et le Noir* one as well?[18] Are *War and Peace* and Goethe's *Elective Affinities* comparable? Which of them is really a novel and which one is not? Are there fixed rules that define an object as a novel and that can exclude other objects from that definition? Who has the authority to decide if a work is a novel or not? Are there objective criteria to distinguish between different art forms and, within them, between different genres? One thing is certain: every normative system, be it art or law, has been challenged both by the question of the definition of the genres—which one might consider as a form of local or regional ontology at play within the larger boundaries of the ontology of art—and by the existence of the extraordinary work and its singularity, which ipso facto questions dominant generic classification.

In general, if the object under assessment is a work of art, the category within which we should assess this work is an artistic genre. If the object is instead a legal litigation, we must refer to judicial trends, which function as categories of

18 Guy De Maupassant as quoted by Mazzoni (2017, 14).

art insofar as they are both descriptive and prescriptive, and can be re-assessed according to the emergence of new extraordinary cases. The concept of 'Art' alone does not seem to be sufficient in order to assess a work of art, since it is too vague to provide us with a suitable standard. We need more fine-grained categories that allow us to assess a work in terms of its form, its function, its features, and its history of making. Artistic genres play this role by influencing and nurturing the expectations towards a work of art.

For example, if an art lover goes to see a sculpture exhibition and finds videos there rather than—let's say—marble or bronze sculptures, she may very well feel puzzled. Reasonably, she might find herself in a position where she has to ponder the following alternative: either assessing such artworks as provoking sculptures or assess them as videos, thereby changing the genre that underlies the judgment. The judgment thus varies depending on which alternative the appreciator chooses, that is, depending on which genre the observer relies on in formulating his or her judgment. Yet this view has been criticized by Jerrold Levinson: categorization, from his perspective, would be a function primarily of the artist's intention.

There have been many attempts to define what a genre is and how it originates. One of the clearest definitions has been given by an prominent philosopher of art, Dominique McIver Lopes; according to his perspective, a genre is a practice that must be performed through a medium, following norms. These norms (he does not specify what form they should have) influence also the appreciation of objects as artworks: they are important both for the artist and for the audience. The creation depends on these norms, since the artists who want to be considered and evaluated within a certain genre and thus within a certain community must follow those norms. Unless they decide to subvert them: this is precisely the "revolutionary" value of extraordinary singularities both in art and in law.

It is unquestionable that, given our current practices, the correct appreciation of a work of art is influenced by categorization. In the absence of considerations related to categories' descriptive and prescriptive function, something would be missing in our aesthetic judgments. Yet, I hasten to add, artistic genres are often redefined by the emergence of extraordinary cases that question the validity of the precedent categorization and description.

Genre definition is a very complex philosophical problem that cannot be addressed here beyond superficially and in relation to the broader theme of this essay. As Enrico Terrone and I suggest, a possible account of the birth of the artistic genre of painting could be the following. Some prehistoric painters started painting the caves and some prehistoric critics appreciated their works. Yet, the appreciation cannot be based on a pre-existing genre, since the genre has not yet been established as a practice, nor as a category. The prehistoric critics just appreciate the cave paintings as signs or objects, but not as paintings. Indeed, it is undoubtable that the genre of painting comes from this basic non-genre-based appreciation. In other words, the first critics only deploy an aesthetic appreciation, not an artistic appreciation. They appreciate the painting in the same way that they could appreciate the shape of a tree or the colour of the sky. Their appreciation is independent from any notion of genre. Nevertheless, such an appreciation creates expectations concerning new objects that are capable of eliciting a similar enjoyment. Here is where painting as an artistic genre begins. The expectations and the interactions among the primitive community select a system of features of the prehistoric painting as *normative* for the forthcoming paintings and these are required to elicit a similar enjoyment.[19]

As for what concerns the role played by singular works like *Brillo Box* in the definition of new genres or in the redefinition of preexisting genres, I am sure that nothing can be created as an exemplar or as an original "first instance" of a new category. A work cannot be created *as* an example, nothing originates as an example: when it is created, it is simply a particular object. Similarly, when a judge utters the first sentences of a decision that becomes, afterwards, revolutionary and paradigmatic, he or she might expect some reaction from that performative moment—but nobody can be entirely certain about the reception and the appreciation of something as extraordinary a priori.

The singularity can *become* an exemplary case because of its extraordinary features and this is how it later becomes a norm of production of similar works (in art) and a model of reference for similar decisions (in law). This happens only by virtue of the fact that the singularity is (or has been) appreciated within a community as extraordinary. Genres have an origin and can undergo changes, which are triggered by new (extraordinary) works that acquire exemplarity by virtue of negotiations within the genre itself: the extraordinary value is thus the product of the relationship with what is considered "ordinary". The first ready-mades became exemplary by leading to a negotiation of the norms constituting a defined artistic genre within contemporary art.

The extraordinary singularities are such also because they are *rare*. If any new creation of any artist everywhere in the world could challenge the definition of an artistic genre, art would not be such an established normative discourse and would instead be a weird and chaotic melting pot with no identity. It is in undoubtable that most of the works belonging to a genre are not exemplary works that are capable of reshaping the genre: they are singular

19 Condello and Terrone (2017).

instances, in other words tokens or *exemplars* (and not *exempla*)—representing that genre in a much weaker sense, because they succeed in complying with the expectations established by that very genre. The reason is that genres, just like many other historical practices, exhibit a high degree of stability. Abiding by the norms of a genre is much easier than changing them: though ordinary and extraordinary are relational concepts, being extraordinary is still more difficult than being ordinary.

Particularly works belonging to avant garde movements tend to constitute attempts to challenge the descriptions and prescriptions about genres: Duchamp's *Fountain* challenges the norms of visual art, Cage's *4'33"* challenges the norms of music, Monteiro's *Branca de neige* challenges the norms of film. For what concerns the challenges of the new and extraordinary singularities that question a preexisting genre classification, it is important to distinguish the different consequences that such challenges might produce.[20] Indeed, they can be rejected, as it was the case with Monteiro's film that, because it consisted of nothing but a soundtrack and a completely white screen, was not financed by the Portuguese government, because it could not be treated like a movie (though it had nevertheless been appreciated by a restricted community of *cinéphiles*). But the challenges of the extraordinary can also be accepted, as in the case of Cage's *4'33'*, which contributed to modifying the normative assets of music. If we are to establish whether a hypothesized genre actually exists, we must necessarily turn towards the experience of classification of a specific object within or outside that genre. Yet, some genres can have a relevant role in the creation and the appreciation of works of art even if that role is not explicitly recognized.[21]

The tension between ordinary and extraordinary in art is thus relevant because it is creative. If, on the one hand, genres influence the creation and appreciation of artworks, on the other hand these principles can be questioned, defined or redefined by the emergence of artistic singularities questioning the dominant definition of a given genre. The philosophical relevance of such an issue finds evidence in the history of the philosophy of art: many of its key texts could be read as attempts to define what a genre is, how it originates, and how it connects with concrete examples. Aristotle's *Poetics* is an account of narration as a genre that goes across literature and theater, and Nietzsche's *The Birth of Tragedy from the Spirit of Music* also aims at building a genealogy of a genre, tragedy, which is understood as a spin-off from a pre-existing genre: music.

20 Condello and Terrone (2017, 43).
21 Cavell (1996).

In his first famous work, Nietzsche provides us with an interesting and nuanced discussion of the possibilities of a genre's evolution, which he clearly understands as non-linear. He tracks the changes in the normative content of tragedy precisely when this genre departs from its origins and is reshaped by extraordinary, unique, and exemplary works, in particular those by Euripides. Then, he shows that some exemplary works, such as Wagner's operas, can even generate a "revolutionary-conservative" move within genre classification, since they are capable of bringing a genre back to its original normative arrangement, which had been (in the meantime) betrayed by subsequent changes:

> Artistic genres have a birth and a life, and they also have a death, and even a resurrection. Genres are brought to life by exemplarity and kept alive by normativity. The reality of a genre is inextricable from its historicity.
> CONDELLO and TERRONE, 2017, 46

3.1 Defining the Extraordinary

The extraordinary object challenges the definition of art by showing its limits: similarly, the extraordinary case (or *cas extraordinaire* as Yan Thomas defined it) in law, by questioning the definition of legal concepts, shows the limits of legal normativity. What appears to be new and unexpected for a certain order creates a crisis that might lead to a redefinition of the categories of art and of genre classification. In normative orders such as art and law, extraordinary cases are thus important because they can be read as a possibility to iterate and repeat what is known or as a possibility to create a different definition of an artistic genre or of a jurisprudential trend and of a legal concept.

Extraordinary cases play a constitutive role in normative practices for what pertains both their emergence and their evolution. In this sense, they are recurrent episodes in the history of a normative practice. The very essence of normative orders lies in the fact that they can be—and generally they are—questioned by the new and unexpected; in other words, by the extraordinary in relation to the established order of categories and of norms of definition. In a certain way, the existence of these normative orders is realized through a sort of psychoanalytic process of individuation caused by all the crises that the order goes through because of the emergence of extraordinary cases. The life of art and law *as* normative orders is thus a long-lasting series of changes of paradigm, or of confirmations, most of which originate in extraordinary artworks or in extraordinary jurisprudential conflicts and cases.[22] The possibility

22 See on this Kuhn (1962).

of the emergence of a potentially questionable singularity is a core aspect of normativity.

The individuation of the content of art or of the definition of legal concepts goes through phases, crises, redefinitions. As philosopher Tiziana Andina well explains in her paper "Exemplarity in Contemporary arts":

> [Warhol] felt that the traditional forms of art had become inadequate to express the deeper meaning of the 20th century. His idea was that a common chair could say something about the world in more effective ways than a traditional painting ever could—even if it was a good one. So he began to produce works that looked like ordinary objects rather than extraordinary paintings.
>
> ANDINA 2018, 6

The result of such a revolutionary attitude was the creation of extraordinary objects, and this needed to be appreciated and understood in order for people to recognize those objects *as* works of art.

Ordinary objects like soap-pad boxes, though difficult to evaluate and to appreciate in the context from which they emerged, became (at least according to Arthur Danto) symbols of the 20th century and thus they became exemplary for their extraordinary and groundbreaking character. Yet if we were to list the reasons why *Brillo Box* was considered extraordinary, the answers could still be questionable nowadays. The exemplary force of similar works of art proves that their extraordinary character is not given by the content or by the material or the technique, but it is instead the consequence of a much more complex system of reasons that make them extraordinary and exemplary.

Usually, at an ontological level, works of art are supposed to appear as special items, clearly different from ordinary items such as, for instance, soap-pad boxes. Warhol's extraordinary creations challenge and even contradict this general rule. Such artefacts question the normative order precisely because they show that even an ordinary item which apparently has nothing special can be used or understood as something extraordinary. Before Duchamp or Warhol, there was no category in which objects like soap-pads or urinals could be classified. The expression-category "ready-made" created a space for the classification and the recognition of many other objects after these first ones. Basically, the new genre originated when the need to define the extraordinary emerged. In the choice between creativity and repetition, the first ready-mades illustrated the force of repetition, which could also gain extraordinary value if used by a specific artist in a specific context.

3.2 Emerging Genres and Trends

It is around the definition of new works, cases, and in general of new singularities that—at a general level—ways of conceiving art and of conceiving legal concepts evolve. In jurisprudence, the extraordinary case is such because it has the capacity to destabilise a concept or theory that is considered valid within a legal system. Consider the following example. *Google Spain*[23] led the European Court of Justice to (re)define the idea of privacy according to the standards of the web era and, likewise, in the United States cases such as *US v. Jones*[24] have overturned a precedent idea of private life, and consequently have led to define also actions like "search" and "seizure" anew.

In front of what had not been foreseen, a normative order like law is pushed to proceed reflectively through a redefinition of its own limits. Without a new, temporary representation of the actions and concepts that converge in the definition of "privacy" or "property", a new jurisprudential trend cannot be established. Such a trend will influence similar cases until the emergence of a new, groundbreaking standard that embodies more, or better, the representation of the same concepts. With the due differences, cases such as *Google Spain,* that established the right to be forgotten in relation to the internet, or as *Brown v. Board of Education*, resemble the extraordinary artworks and pose similar questions of changes in demarcation and definition. These cases, before becoming standards for further cases, that is, landmark decisions, created doubts and posed questions about the correct characterization of legal concepts. Such concepts were going through a crisis because of a societal change.

Likewise, it seems that with *Brillo Box* Warhol wanted to question the very idea that an artwork, in order to be appreciated as such, must present aesthetic features that distinguish it from commonplace objects. In both fields, art and law, the extraordinary singularity has the capacity to produce an earthquake. Joseph Margolis, in his *The Importance of Being Earnest about the Definition and Metaphysics of Art*, writes:

---

23 *Google Spain SL, Google Inc. v Agencia Española de Protección de Datos, Mario Costeja González* (2014) is a decision by the European Court of Justice. The decision held that an internet search engine operator (Google, in this case) is responsible for the processing of personal information which appears on web pages published by third parties.

24 *United States v. Jones*, 132 S.Ct. 945 (2012) is a decision of the American Supreme Court which held for the first time that installing a GPS tracking device on a vehicle and using the device to monitor the vehicle's movements constitutes a search under the Fourth Amendment. The case is considered revolutionary since until this decision the legal concept of "search" used in the Fourth Amendment would include actions such as tapping, but not yet following through a GPS system.

> Duchamp threw the artworld and the aesthetician's sense of the "artworld" into disarray; Warhol petitioned for admission to the established artworld.
>
> MARGOLIS 2010, 216

In brief, he claims that definitions are provisional, given for a purpose, and need to be flexible enough to accommodate new and inventive cases. Margolis underlines that Greenberg recognized the danger to Modernism that Duchamp posed, and Danto found in Warhol a simple way to recover a supposedly changeless order beneath the threatening scatter.

The disarray mentioned by Margolis resembles the disarray that precedes the decision of extraordinary cases that might become "impact cases" in law, that is to say decisions that function as standards within a specific field of law. And this common disarray is indeed natural: both artistic and legal concepts are in fact characterized by a familiarity to what Hart called an "open texture" or, similarly, to what Wittgenstein has defined as family resemblance concepts. For such concepts, it is impossible to find definitive common traits and for this reason the definition of genres is dynamic and influenced by the emergence of the extraordinary. Margolis continues:

> We cannot possibly know a priori whether "art" lends itself to essential definition. In fact, there is no essential definition of "definition", unless [...] for a "special purpose"! [...] Also, "essential" definitions may be merely nominal as distinct from "real" (or realist); and what Weitz might regard as failed essential definitions of the realist kind may, in Wittgenstein's tolerant sense, actually be successful in their own way (that is, "for a special purpose").
>
> MARGOLIS 2010, 219

The open texture of "art" and of legal concepts makes both art and law permeable and thus extremely sensitive to the extraordinary character of groundbreaking artworks and of landmark cases: the revolutionary force of the relationship between ordinary and extraordinary in art and law is due to this characteristic nature of these two fields. Open concepts are corrigible and emendable, and it is impossible to state necessary and sufficient conditions for their application.

According to such an understanding of art, it would seem impossible to give a definition of it and of artistic genres once for all: such an approach is indeed skeptical towards any definition.[25]

---

25 Adajian (2016).

Such a skeptical approach to the definition of art leaves room for the extraordinary case to acquire the force of a norm. Artistic genres and jurisprudential trends are open, since new cases can extend or reduce their scope. The *definiendum* in both art and law is unstable to capture. In another work, Margolis appears to be even more of a pragmatist, when he writes:

> [...] genre properties are projected and idealized from craft practices; they are not normally separable from their aggregated exemplars in the way physical predicates tend to be. Genre distinctions are not antecedently defined abstract predicates instantiated contingently among randomly tested particulars; they are collectively manifested exemplars of an age or *Geist* or something of the sort.
>
> MARGOLIS 2010, 116

Basically, artistic genres (like jurisprudential trends, as I try to demonstrate in *Part 2*) capture the open texture of the concepts of art: genres are classifications aimed at identifying the changing saliences of the historical formations grasped materially and concretely through the singularities and not by formal definitions.

A similar, "realist", conception of genres is illustrated by Gregory Currie, who claims that genre classification is mainly a historical operation: genres are classified through the historical judgements about them according to the singular extraordinary instances that emerge as first instances of new genres, like *Fountain* or *Brillo Box*. According to the definition given by Gregory Currie, genres are ways of grouping different instances and narratives into kinds—for a specific reason, i.e. to group different works according to an internal similarity (style, material, form, etc.) or according to the historical value given to a certain kind of works: for instance, Jacobean tragedies are all related to patterns of mutual influence.[26]

According to Currie, the historical criterion for something to be a genre is the most important one: in the birth of a new genre, the acceptance by the audience concurs with other aspects in judging whether an artwork falls into a new genre; what is crucial is also how the new object came about and how it was presented to the collectivity.

In this sense, the function of art critics (in the case of artistic discourse) and of jurists and commentators (in the case of legal discourse) is central to the understanding of how the definition of a new genre or trend works. New genres are basically the historical responses to the need of classifying and defining

26 Currie (2004, 48–49).

an object which does not fall in the system of genres and definitions already accepted. Basically, new genres are ways of including the extraordinary within the ordinary. By defining a new genre, for instance: "ready-made", the new and unknown objects find their place within an organized system of definitions.

I have already pointed out that skeptical positions towards genre classification claim that the very notion of genre is hostile to appreciation: this type of classification shows very well how normativity is constantly redefined in connection to the historical context. Artistic genres—and, similarly, jurisprudential trends—have the power to create expectations. Even though they can be considered as floating categories, they have the power to define what the audience expects from determined types of artworks or of jurisprudential cases. Currie writes:

> Questions about what is a genre for a community are contingent and empirical; we cannot know, merely on the basis of our competence with the concept of a given genre, whether works in a given genre are produced in this community. [...] It is tempting to say that a work belongs to a genre just in case it possesses the associated set of genre-features. But we cannot say this. Membership in a genre depends on more than simply exhibiting the relevant genre-features; it depends on those features having a certain salience for the community.
>
> CURRIE 2004, 48

Though the questions about the genre are empirical, what counts is that in this kind of classificatory operation there are two levels that coexist: the descriptive and the normative. The descriptive level is where the patterns of expectation prevailing within a community are defined. The normative level is where genre classification produces effects on further works because it indicates how they should be in order to fall within that class or category.

How exactly does the singular artwork or jurisprudential case emerge *as* exemplary? How and for what reasons is it capable of questioning the validity of a genre by creating the possibility of a new genre? In a recent essay, convincing answers to these questions have been offered by drawing on a philosophy of language's famous debate on indexicals.[27] Indexicals can indeed be considered as paradigmatic singular terms which single out individuals or predicates that designate properties. When I utter the sentence "my table is like that", pointing at a particular table, in that singularity (the specific table I am indicating) the

27 Terrone (2018). Among the fundamental philosophical references on indexicals, Strawson (1959); Strawson (1962); Strawson (1966); Strawson (1979); Kripke (1980).

predicate ("to be like this", so maybe wooden or marble) is shown by a specific individual and is not defined by a reference to an abstract characteristic (like in the case "my table is made of wood"). In some sense, the extraordinary singularity becomes exemplary not for a specific material, or for a contextual character, but because in that specific moment and space it is capable of representing a contingent need of definition for something new. And it does so by pointing beyond itself and yet remaining a singular instance. The extraordinary instance is a sort of "virtual finger" that transforms the singularity into a potential model for further cases.

The singularity that, because of its extraordinary nature, becomes an exemplary case that leads to a redefinition of a genre or to the creation of a new, different genre, emerges because it has the capacity to indicate something beyond itself. For instance, *Brillo Box* indicated the need to redefine the relationship between special and extraordinary objects and artworks; *Brown v. Board of Education* indicated that civil rights in America were not recognized correctly before that decision. These and similar extraordinary singularities point towards something beyond themselves. They thus overcome the distinction between individuals and properties, since they are—in the terms used by Strawson—individuals used to indicate a property.

Singularities can also be surprising: they are fine-tuned to a degree that cannot be anticipated by the generality of an abstract norm or concept (the idea of book is not as detailed as the book I have here in front of me, which is one copy of one specific work). The "surprise-effect" is a consequence of the contingent details, which transform the singularity into something extraordinary as opposed to what is perceived as, or expected to be, ordinary.[28] There is a profound solidarity between the extraordinary singularity (or case) and its capacity to become an original and exemplary model for other cases within the same genre or trend. The singularity emerges from reality and has a direct and immediate relationship with it; as a matter of fact, it emerges because there is some kind of limit in the ordinary character of reality and it is in reaction to this limit that the singularity emerges as exemplary and extraordinary.

The extraordinary case is a reaction to a preexisting order. As stated before, if there was no ordinary there would be no extraordinary. The limits and obstacles of reality are the necessary condition for the extraordinary singularity to emerge. By its very coming into existence, the individual case indicates the possibility of a transformation: the possibility of what until then had not been imagined.

---

28 Ferraris (2016).

Part 2: The Extraordinary in Law

In legal theory, rhetorics, figurative language, and the role of casuistry have always been among the most relevant themes in discussion. Recently, Peter Goodrich has proposed a thought-provoking account of the exemplary jurisprudential case in terms of its methodological impact both at a rhetorical and at an epistemic level.[29] In order to understand and discuss the relationship between ordinary and extraordinary in law, let me first introduce some features of juridical normativity for which the singular case plays a crucial role.

How could we define law and its function in society? In what sense can the particular (extraordinary) case be considered important for a thorough understanding of juridical normativity? Law can be defined as a system of more or less broad rules issued by those institutions that have the competence and power to issue those rules. Juridical rules can be more or less clear: it depends on the language used by the legislator and also by other factors like, for instance, the context of reception of the rules.

In general, the content of the norms can be clarified through adjudication: it is in the moment of the decision—and thus when norms are applied—that their general nature is measured with the particular nature of the facts, of the events, and of the proper names and stories at stake in the decision of each case. Law is thus, by nature, riddled with contradiction, complexity, and uncertainty. The reciprocal measurement between norms and facts is at the centre of the main theoretical questions regarding law. That is to say, it is at the centre of questions of interpretation, application, realism, positivism, and similar approaches that reflect different dispositions towards the same relationship, i.e. the relationship between the normative system and reality.[30]

There are inevitable paradoxes between these two contiguous but separate domains of norms and facts: there is inevitable (and permanent) tension between a social system of rule generation, the interpretation of such rules and their application. The existence of law, both in case-based systems (like the common law) and in code-based systems (like the civil law), has always been characterised by the internal tensions between these opposed forces. Desmond Manderson has described law's existence in this manner as its "polarity".[31] According to Manderson, juridical normativity is intrinsically polar because

29 Goodrich (2017).
30 Condello and Mason (in print, forthcoming 2019).
31 Manderson (2012).

its existence is everywhere characterized by the presence of conflicting forces in search for a principle of common measurement.[32]

It is undoubtable, on the one hand, that the existence of the law is intrinsically connected to those tensions. It is also evident, on the other hand, that the law often resolves the tension between abstract norms and real situations by making reference to singular exemplary cases, in which polarities collapse and are reconciled. The singular cases that for some extraordinary feature can function as models and "embodied norms" are on the edge of normativity. As already mentioned in the first section about art, a singularity becomes exemplary precisely because it questions the separation between ordinary and extraordinary in law. As Manderson argues, those two edges touch one another and reconcile in the singular case. The case, in turn, emerges as extraordinary because, in it, the force of the particularity and the force of generality coexist. The extraordinary singularity like *Brown v. Board of Education* is thus, first and foremost, the space of encounter of opposing poles.

Jurists are therefore capable, through the use of exemplarity, of inhabiting the personification of legal theory. In some sense, approaching law through the relationship between ordinary and extraordinary invites to imagine a new rhetorical approach to law that focuses on the central role of the case. This approach places at the centre of its interests the nature of law and its confrontation with singular experiences. Such an approach might be said to be inspired by a sort of modernist taste in legal theory centered around the detail, the particular feature, and the specificity of each singular experience: in other words, this focus on the case reflects a need to interrogate a new perspective in legal methodology that includes, systematically, the contrast with the singular experiences.

A new rhetorical approach to law focused on singularity might offer an opportunity to question the authority of legal discourse within society, starting from the juridical problem (like the Medieval *quaestio*) posed by the singularity. The singularity has a privileged and yet conflictual relation to the general norm, and because of this it challenges universal claims or assumptions. The exemplary case is interesting to observe both in common law and in civil law systems, starting from the crucial role played by the case in the illustration of how normative commitments work. The normative universe is in fact held together by interpretive commitments. These commitments determine what law means. Not just what law means in general, but what law could mean in a specific context and according to the commitments of the individuals who take part to the same interpretive community. Such a process of objectification of

32 Manderson (2012).

norms makes norms more accessible, because objects are what is presented in front of the observer while it is impossible to fully understand a concept. Now, quite obviously, the objectification cannot be based only on concepts: it entails the use of narratives. The exemplary case embodies both the narrative and the norm, so it allows for an encounter between these two grammars: it contributes to enrich the interpretability of norms because it enlarges or narrows their content.[33] This dynamic interrelation between norms and narratives is one in which law does not simply demand its supporting narrative, but also becomes itself a narrative of multiple possible worlds of ends and means; not simply *nomos* and narrative, but *nomos* as narrative and narrative as *nomos*.[34]

As noted by Alessandro Ferrara, the force of the singularity emerges in contexts of normative pluralism:[35] the existence of law measures itself every day with a plurality of values that illustrate multiple ways in which social and political systems can be (and, actually, are) regulated—and all of these ways are in turn connected to the culture(s) characterizing a specific historical context. As a matter of fact, law originates from society and regulates the same society from which it originates: tension, contradiction, and reflexivity are thus features that essentially characterize law's nature.

The relation between legal and extra-legal systems is mirrored in the existence of legal norms: social reality is in fact necessary in order for the law to exist from an ontological point of view. This entails that law must always have a double code: on the one hand, legal rules must formally possess a prescriptive attitude; yet, on the other hand, law must also be given meaning contextually and by the community which it regulates. Law's polarity also deals with this double bind between law and society, that is between the forms of the law and the needs, the desires, and the changing values that populate reality. It regulates the social world, yet is given effectiveness and meaning by that very social world and by its practices. The law is structurally incapable, in and of itself, of comprehending the myriad of cultural, economic and power-based complexities of human existence. Equally, the law's reaction to the single example of narrative would provide a comprehensible reaction, in concrete form, to the logic of that social system, which it might be capable of extrapolating into a more general set of norms and meanings within that field. This is clearly an idealised vision of this process: the law might fail to grasp certain things about the world it is seeking to regulate; in turn, the world might be incapable of transposing the outcome of the single case into more general practices of meanings.

33 Condello and Mason (in print, forthcoming 2019).

34 Fraade (2005).

35 Ferrara (2008, 18).

However, without the possibility of the emergence of the case, and of the extraordinary case in particular, the law and its social function would remain pretty unrelated: the law would simply be a set of ignored interpellations of the world which it was, concretely and in truth, incapable of understanding. The extraordinary case, with its capacity to call into question and even contradict the general norm, offers a glimpse on the space in between law (order) and reality (where the possibility of the extraordinary originates). The extraordinary singularities—the exemplary jurisprudential cases—are individual stories making up singular encounters and, as such, they are the engine animating and defining the law's ontological essence. In other words, by drawing on legal realist Roscoe Pound, they live in the tension between *law in books* and *law in action*.

The meanings of the law are "forced" into conversation precisely by the singular cases, i.e. by the concrete instances where the narratives of the law and the narratives of the world face one another. The fact that the singular case can interpellate the general level of the regulation is crucial for the nature of the law and its operation, in particular with regard to law's various polarities, for example, between particular and general, between concrete and abstract, and between extraordinary and ordinary. These polarities are indeed basic for the life of the law, which otherwise would not have any meaning. For this reason, making sense of individual instances and cases is crucial for the stability of the function of the law within society, a stability which should be continuous despite the gaps separating normativity and reality, as well as ordinary and extraordinary. Legal normativity lives in the tension, contrast, and encounter between these heterogeneous dimensions.

Since norms—be them general and abstract norms or precedent cases performing the function of norms—will never "correspond" completely to what occurs in reality, the extraordinary singularities are concrete instances of the life of the law because they show how much law is related to the "measurement", the containment and the limitation of the world.[36] The case is the space "in between" where, through individual stories, the law encounters real names, real times and spaces; every singular case is the area of such an encounter. Yet, extraordinary cases force the law more concretely into a simultaneously introspective and outward looking act of projecting its abstractions onto the world, while questioning—at the same time—whether it can justify its demands.[37]

Extraordinary cases like *Obergefell* for gay marriage rights, or *Brown* for nondiscrimination, combine different aspects: a series of fact-events, a series of

36 Thévenin (2017).

37 Condello and Mason (in print, forthcoming 2019).

actions, and the specific value of the actions within a context.[38] For instance, *Obergefell* is extraordinary because it happened in 2015 and because at that time the rights of same-sex couples were at the centre of public debate and, most importantly, because before that case the "norm" or accepted "order" did not reflect the needs of juridical recognition of same-sex couples. *Brown v. Board of Education* (1954) was considered extraordinary when it was released because, at that time, the inequalities between African-American citizens and non-African-American citizens were still institutionalized. Societal needs to abolish those inequalities had become almost irresistible. *Brown*, the singular extraordinary case, interpellated the general law through its specificity. That is to say: by establishing that separate public schools for black and white students were unequal, that particular case overruled the precedent decision in *Plessy v. Ferguson* (1896), according to which the law of separation was not to be considered unconstitutional. The particular narrative of *Brown v. Board of Education* became an *exemplum* because it intercepted a specific need of that time and it did it at a specific timing: in some sense, it functioned as a *kairòs*, i.e. as the exact or proper instant that shows the course of time and the evolution of normativity through time. *Brown*, like other extraordinary and exemplary decisions such as *Obergefell* or, at a European level, *Google Spain* (EJC, 2014), grasps the *Zeitgeist* by embodying a due timing because of its story and because of the particular gesture performed by the parts in the case: all those specific features make it extraordinary. Exemplarity is also defined in relation to the historical moment of emergence of the singular case. The relationship between ordinary and extraordinary in law thus shows that time plays an important role in the polarity between facts and norms.[39]

When confronted with the extraordinary and unexpected, the law is placed into a position whereby it *must* justify its own application, either in terms of the justifiability of its content, or through some second-order justification of the application of its content despite its inherent injustice. In this way, the extraordinary case, the fleeting encounter with other social spheres, is a mechanism by means of which the law is forced to engage in a form of introspection and self-reflection. When the law is confronted with the singularity, it is necessarily faced with the question: is this outcome acceptable? The polarity of ordinary and extraordinary collapses in the law's inevitable reliance on the singular case.

38 Condello (2018).

39 Cover (1983–1984).

1 *The Original Need for Singular Norms*

Law is not the only normative order that makes use of extraordinary singularities in order to describe and to prescribe a type of behaviour. As a matter of fact, in order to distinguish the good from the evil, or in order to define a virtue, we often refer to specific cases of people that we know personally, or cases that we have heard in stories or books. This attitude was common in antiquity, and in particular already in the Greek world. For instance, in many of Plato's earlier dialogues, Socrates interrogates the Athenians about the nature of some virtues: in the *Laches*, he investigates courage, in the *Eutbypbro*, he asks the Athenians about piety; in the *Republic*, he is interested in the nature of justice.

If *dike* is understood as a general order of justice at a universal level (literally: "at the level of the universe"), the *dikaios* is the single man that—for his extraordinary capacity to embody that kind of order of justice—is considered as a model of justice, as an *exemplum* of justice. The *dikaios* is extraordinary and representative because he knows the universal order and does not violate its norms but, instead, he embodies them in a very peculiar way. He distinguishes himself from the other men because he embodies human features that correspond to the value of justice and he does so in an extraordinary way.

This is the case of the embodied norm *par excellence*, Jesus Christ, who recognizes the positive order of written norms of the scribes and offers as an alternative, on a parallel level, his unique normativity, the normativity of a form of life ("but I say unto you"). Such a normativity aims to speak a universal language, and yet remains also in contact with the transience of the life of a man, that will eventually and necessarily die. When radicalized, this perspective might lead to a position of ethical intellectualism, according to which people will do what is right just if they truly understand what is right: thus, in order to be performed, virtues must be understood through the short distance created by the particular life of the extraordinary individual, in which we can recognize ourselves and that gives us a privileged access to the content of the universal prescription.[40] From the perspective of ethical intellectualism (or Socratic intellectualism), what motivates actions and what creates the perception that something should be done in a certain way—is a cognitive state: if we understand "good" or "courage" through the *exemplum* of an extraordinary man like Socrates, who embodies either one of those features in an extraordinary way, it will be easier to perform those values concretely. Tautological as it might sound, the extraordinary wisdom of Socrates and his exemplarity are interconnected. He is an *exemplum* of wisdom because his wisdom is extraordinary:

40 Parry (2014).

he emerges as extraordinary and differentiates himself from other men because of this outstanding capacity to represent wisdom.

The original need for particular models, specifically in the legal realm, is rooted in the way normativity functions, and in particular in the connection between juridical normativity and the society where it emerges. The singular extraordinary case invites a reflection on how laws can be binding. As a matter of fact, norms aim at influencing and regulating human behaviour, so the question about the need for extraordinary singular cases that can function as norms questions the prescriptive value of norms. Sylvie Delacroix, who has worked on the normative force of legal norms, wrote:

> How can law bind us, if it is contingent upon the changing wills and desires of whoever happens to hold political power?
> Underlying this concern is the idea that law's claim to bindingness is only viable if some form of necessity can commend law as a desirable framework for the organisation of our society [...].
>
> DELACROIX 2006, ix

The relationship between ordinary and extraordinary in law is connected to the very meaning of the concept of "normativity": such a concept is obviously pervasive in legal discourse, since law is first and foremost a system of norms. Following Delacroix, one could say that, in law, normativity indicates a section of human experience which is not directly related to what is in the world, but makes claims (or is obliged to follow claims) about what the world should be like or ought to be.[41]

There are many sources of normativity and positive norms are certainly the most common. Yet, as I have tried to argue by making reference to the field of art, the term 'normative' can be used to indicate a very diversified range of statements. Regulations, directives, clauses and general principles, international conventions, decisions by lower courts, decisions by higher courts, precedent cases are all sources of juridical normativity—and the list is far from complete.

Recognizing the existence of all those forms of normativity requires that the rules are respected: otherwise, if they were not recognized nor respected, we would not talk about legal norms. 'Normative' is used alternatively to describe the fact that law can be used for guidance or to describe the fact that law's requirements must be deemed obligatory by a part of the population. In the first,

41 Delacroix (2006, x and xi).

'normative' refers to a feature inherent to the prescriptive attitude of law; in the second instance, 'normative' is defined by reference to its obligatory character and by its capacity to bind, effectively, human behaviours. On the one hand, the first instance describes a definition of law that can refer to a general and abstract prescription; on the other hand, the second instance requires a direct comparison with the singular cases. From this second point of view, the "life of the law" is more relevant than the theory of law: where can this "life" be seen, observed, in action? In the extraordinary singularity—just like the power of the State is perceived by the individual in the moment of the concrete interpellation by the police man, as claimed by Luis Althusser. The extraordinary case *interpellates* juridical normativity.

Concretely, the singularity does something that the general norm cannot do: it shows the existence of interests and values that are (or might be) conflicting with the general norm, and shows that they can also have their validity. The singularity thus illustrates new and different reasons for action, which are the foundation of every normative order: if it is not validated and legitimized by some reasons for action, the normative order has less "*prise*" on reality. The extraordinary case, on the contrary, is all constructed around the specific aspects of the singular narrative and, at an individual level, it tells a story and the reasons for action related to *that* individual narrative. When the interests, values and reasons for action shown by the extraordinary singularity are stronger than the reasons described by the general proposition, the extraordinary singular case acquires normative value and can be used as a model for further, similar, cases. Obviously, the concept of legal normativity needs more than mere reasons in order to be accounted for; yet, without those reasons it would be impossible to see the emergence of a norm in the case. In other words, singular cases can produce motives for actions that—at least sometimes—supersede positive norms. Such motives are so powerful since they have an immediate grasp on reality that abstract norms lack.

The extraordinary case in law also illustrates two functions of legal norms that are usually only described theoretically: guidance and obligation. Law's capacity to bind us is rooted into a project aiming to foster a certain way of living together. This project is in turn bound to change, evolving along the shifting (and conflicting) values characterising a pluralist society. The extraordinary case contains all the aspects that give body and force to legal normativity. It shows: (i) that prescriptions reflect a certain view of the world; (ii) that legal normativity is always contextual; (iii) that legal normativity is validated by the same community from which it emerges, thus that the content of norms might change in time:

> If one is to give any weight to the ideal of civic responsibility, the answer has to be framed in terms of legitimacy: the reasons provided by law are conclusive, and thus gain obligatory force, if law is deemed to promote a set of moral and prudential concerns essential to a 'good' way of living together. Once confronted with the demands of morality or prudence, the reasons provided by law may, for a particular individual at a particular time, fail to give rise to an obligation. This need not rob law of its normative force.
>
> DELACROIX 2006, xiv

The extraordinary singularity like those mentioned as examples must reflect some dominating value and thus proves how law's power to bind us is *concomitant* to a *project* aiming to foster a certain way of living together. The fact that this project is embodied in the singularity entails that the project is not everlasting: it is, instead, bound to change.

From this perspective, the singularity contributes to show that questioning and debating are necessary in order to maintain legal legitimacy: changing societal values demand diverse ways of conceiving notions of—among the others—"justice", "equity", and "prudence". Looking at legal normativity from casuistry allows us to imagine a genealogical perspective and overcome the risk of attributing fixed and determinate groundings to legal propositions. Such fixity, especially today, seems impossible: the sources of normative accounts on our lives are multiplied by the various communication devices and circulate more quickly and more easily. Though not devoid of risks, this version of legal anti-foundationalism opens up the possibility of a dialogue between the legal and the non-legal world and actually proves the theoretical importance of interdisciplinary studies on law (like law and literature, law and art, etc.).

The "original" need for singular models reflects its force also on the law: it is from such an inclination that we can understand why law is capable of binding us, according to a project that lies behind the concrete norms and that is nourished by societal and cultural requests. The singularity has an allegorical value because it stands for something else, like for instance the extraordinary cases that are such because they are the object of strategic litigations for fundamental rights. Law can actually be a way to achieve a better way of living together, and to commit ourselves to it.

Summarizing, the extraordinary in law leads us to focus on two main points:

(i) the sources of legal validity: do they lie in preexisting, posited principles, or are they constantly negotiated? The answer is that those forces resemble the double equilibrium of sources for which Jesus Christ can say that there are written norms, and yet he addresses the people to say something else, or something more.

(ii) Law's capacity to bind us independently of the project it is meant to serve, which questions the limits of law in relation to other normative orders such as religion, morality, etc.

2 *Extraordinary Cases in Roman Jurisprudence*

The practice of referring to singular exemplary narratives, events, or cases was very common in Ancient Rome.[42] To begin, the *ars oratoria* and the *ars rhetorica* make constant reference to the *exemplum*: Quintilian suggests that there is no better way to learn about virtues—such as "courage" and "justice"—than to read the stories of famous men and women who lived before us. The achievements and deeds of ancient heroes are the first secular experience of the reference to embodied norms. Proper names play a fundamental role in the education of young Romans: loyalty, courage, continence—are all values incorporated in the extraordinary lives of evocative men like the Curii, the Fabricii, and others. The heroic figures are definitely extraordinary: they resist, they conquer, they can be tortured and yet survive, they stand firm against the enemy. They sacrifice themselves for others: as the other extraordinary singularities that are the center of this work, they contrast an "order", that is, a structured and persistent system of values. They do so through a different *ratio*, a different system of truth production and a different form. Young Romans would learn about good and evil through these figures. Rebecca Langlands writes:

> But what did learning about virtue from such examples actually entail? What kind of access to generalizable knowledge of virtue did these individual and particular exempla provide? Was their role essentially epistemological or rhetorical? Did they actually teach what the concepts of "courage," "justice" and so on meant, or did they rather inspire and clarify?
> LANGLANDS 2015, 68

If the space between the ordinary and the extraordinary mirrors the distinction between the norm and the singular case, and thus also the impossibility of their coexistence, then the extraordinary case also offers a solution of compromise between these two codes: in the singular case—when extraordinary and paradigmatic—norms and facts coexist. The extraordinary case is in fact both exceptional and ordinary, daily, tangible: it is like Jesus Christ, who is constantly oscillating between his transcendent and his bodily nature (and one

42 Langlands (2015).

nature interpellates the other until the very end of his life). The extraordinary singularity claims a new and original validity, its own way of addressing a community both in contrast and in relation with the positive norms. It does so by being the very measure of the positive norms and by showing the limits of their validity, their *katechon*.

The double bind between the singularity and the universal value (or interest) that the singularity embodies recalls the philosophical problem of what comes prior between the chicken and the egg, that is to say between the source and the product of that source which can become a new source itself. This circularity is interrupted by the extraordinary singularity, which gives access to a third space, beyond the space of the egg and the space of the chicken, by incorporating their interaction. The question about the prior value of the norm or of the singular case is actually misleading, as the extraordinary and exemplary case proves. Can the *exempla* function as those normative tools by means of which we first establish what a virtue such as "wisdom" is? Or are they only able to act as reminders of a moral idea that one has already understood and already enacted? Is the concrete action a prerequisite of the existence of a value? Langlands rightly recalls the *Critique of Judgement*, where Kant suggested that while examples bring the abstractions down to earth and serve to make perceptible what the practical law expresses generally, the generalizations and abstractions are always established beforehand by principles and theory:

> I [...] argue [...] that Roman exemplarity does present a particular practical solution to many of the problems with *exempla* that have been identified over the centuries, as a cultural practice that does not usually explicitly address such metaphysical issues but nevertheless seems to acknowledge their implications and to provide a means to negotiate them in real-life ethics. By effectively combining the persuasive function of *exempla* (as exhortations to virtue and models for virtue) with the inculcation of a form of practical wisdom akin to Aristotelian *phronesis*, Roman exemplarity promoted an approach that allowed for critical independence.
>
> LANGLANDS 2015, 69

In Rome, the extraordinary singularity contributes to build a common cultural memory; thanks in particular to Stoicism, Romans believed that the good values (and the values in general) had been understood and inferred by the careful observation of the actions and deeds of singular men who appeared as perfect models. And only from those actions wise men could learn how to behave properly and according to the values dominating at their time, as it emerges from the Letters of Seneca (Sen. Ep. 120.4–5). Each *exemplum* must exemplify a particular abstract idea or value that the learners can access through its particular instance. The instance is extraordinary because it embodies that specific feature, or value, more and better than other instances. This entails that virtues exist in a simple, definable form. The singularity is also interesting because it shows its imperfections: in particular, it shows the impossibility of reaching a complete correspondence between real life scenarios and abstract values and ideals. Thus, the extraordinary case is such not only for its extraordinary features, but also for its extraordinary *limitedness*: that is to say, for its ability to fail and for its proximity to life.

The deeds, the actions might be extraordinary for some reason and in some context, but the singularity always shows flaws. Otherwise it would be a universal, abstract and exact norm (which of course it is not). To go back to the example used in the introduction, Jesus Christ died because of his human nature: that is to say, precisely because of his limits and flaws. The symbols of his passion are blood and scars, the material elements of the human nature. Blood in particular is what conveys life and force but also, when it comes to the surface, the first sign of a problem in the body. The flaws can be hidden by the extraordinary features, but they are part of the contingent nature of the case. In order to be a means of communication of values, in the extraordinary singularity the deeds must be exaggerated: it must be more particular than an ordinary particularity; and the flaws of the actions must be evident. Seneca makes it clear that one does not have access, through *exempla*, to some kind of perfect ideal of virtue: far from it. What one reaches is a very basic and flawed grasp of what a virtue is and, because of this, a more concrete ideal of virtue, an ideal that can be imitated and reproduced.

The process of learning from *exempla* gives access not so much to a range of universal abstractions, as to a culturally agreed body of moral values and models, with all the complexity and contradictions that these entail. Through this process, the average Roman youth can acquire an adequate practical and working knowledge of virtues so as to understand how to act virtuously without needing to be able to state definitively what courage or wisdom are. This theme is recurrent in moral philosophy, epistemology, and logic. Peter Geach defines "Socratic fallacy" the idea that we first need to have a formal and abstract understanding of a concept in order to use it:[43] in the *Eutbypbro* in particular, Socrates claims that it is more important to have a general knowledge of values than to know how to perform them. Geach says that he disagrees with

43 Geach (1972, 36).

those philosophers that refuse to allow that a proper name is a word within a sentence, unless a formal and rigorous definition of the term 'word' is produced. For Geach, who follows the second Wittgenstein and believes in the pragmatic understanding of concepts case by case, formal definitions are only one way of elucidating terms; a set of examples may, in a given case, be more useful didactically than a formal definition.

The link between extraordinary and exemplary singularity is proved by the fact that, in Rome, the concepts of *exemplum* and *exceptio* appear, in the most diverse contexts, to be interconnected.

The exceptional is interconnected with the extraordinary: in both concepts, we find networks of relationships between particular and universal, individual and community, exclusion and inclusion, deduction and induction. Moreover, according to a distinction introduced by Alessandro Ferrara, the exemplary case can either (1) confirm, in some incredible way, a norm (by showing more and better than other instances the content of that norm: so a very well executed sculpture like the *Pietà* by Michelangelo can be considered an exemplary sculpture); or (2) it can undermine the authority of a norm by showing an alternative possibility and an alternative normativity.

The exceptional in this context refers to the first meaning (confirmation) of exemplarity according to Ferrara's definition, while the extraordinary reflects the second one. Both are singular instances that are in a specific connection with the general norm. Both are prefigured by the separative prefix *ex-*, suggestive of a synecdochic (part/whole) relationship. The root of both compounds intensifies the prefix's external orientation: in the one case *emere*, in the other *capere*. In both cases, we find a verb deriving from the semantic field of the action of taking, grasping, selecting, as they can both mean "to take". The elementary meaning of the Latin term *exemplum* defines "*quod e copia rerum aequalium eximitur*" (what is taken from an abundance of comparable items). The earliest evidence documents its basic function as the "sample" of commercial wares.[44] The sample recalls the image of an aesthetic device that shows the characteristics of a category.

Both the *exemplum* and the *exceptio* have a disruptive function: both provoke some kind of earthquake, a distance and a separation from what is considered "ordinary". They both have to do with a condition of inapplicability of a norm that, in itself, had been considered reasonable and valid until then. It is the borders of a positive rationality that the extraordinary instances question: traditionally, the *exceptio* belongs to the defense, it is something that is *opposed* in order to challenge the normal, typical context. For this reason, the

44 Möller (2015, 96).

genuine sphere of influence of the *exceptio* is within the community: it serves to stabilize the social communication of norms. The extraordinary case, on the other hand, indicates the possibility of another normative equilibrium. In other words, as noted already in this book (*Part 1*), the exception challenges the preexisting norm by confirming it, while the extraordinary case creates its own normativity.

In ancient Rome, the *exemplum* performs its functions in different fields, and this transversal nature is of absolute interest from the perspective of juridical knowledge; though its preferred locus may be the *genus iudiciale*, it also unfolds its effects in the *genus deliberativum* and *demonstrativum*, sometimes showing its ethical and sometimes its illustrative value. The singular extraordinary case, the *exemplum*, is used to visualize evidence and also to convince, to demonstrate, and to illustrate.

Historically, Roman lawyers were often challenged by the exceptional and the extraordinary: such a frequency was due to the structure and the organization of the territory. These occasions became particularly recurrent when "Rome" started to indicate both the *urbe* and the huge provincial territories whose juridical systems were different from those of Rome. Again, singularities show their force more effectively in pluralist contexts, where it is difficult to agree on values. Romans drew distinctions of various kinds between urban and provincial contexts and between what they termed formulary and extraordinary procedure.[45] The Latin expression regularly translated "extraordinary", *extra ordinem*, might best be translated "non-ordinary", as it could refer to a number of non-formulary procedures. In the usage of modern specialists of Roman law, this expression is generally invoked to describe a procedure regularly employed in provincial contexts, in which the magistrate inquired into issues of law and fact in one hearing and settled the case himself. The extraordinary emerges when different languages encounter. Singular exemplary cases were considered particularly useful in situations of normative pluralism: in particular, in provincial contexts, case law (and the cases decided by the emperor in particular) was cited by litigants to force the hand of judges.

3 *Uses of the Ordinary–Extraordinary Dichotomy*

In contemporary legal discourse, extraordinary cases like *Google v. Spain* (indicating: right to be forgotten, right to privacy on the internet) or *Obergefell v. Hodges* (indicating: right of same-sex couples to get married) have many functions. First and foremost, they are used by judges and attorneys to prove the validity of a certain reasoning and balance of interests. So we can say that

45 Ando (2015, 111 ff).

they still have a rhetorical and persuasive value, though less formalized than in antiquity. The exemplary cases create a model of reference for identifying societal values. Thanks to the public debates that they generate and from which they emerge, such cases show the limits of juridical normativity when a specific right or value (e.g. freedom of religion) clashes against another right or value (e.g. security or dignity).

The exemplarity of such cases is the consequence of various factors: the clarity with which they present such conflicts, their capacity to undermine a precedent order and to impose a new one, their innovative force, that is, their capacity to push a court to recognize for the first time a particular right. These cases embody a peculiar form of normativity embedded in the extra-legal reality, and yet they have an unquestionable juridical force: they have an influence on public discourse. To put it brutally, extraordinary singularities make natural law emerge in the form of the "just" reason in the specific case: the singular narrative in the singular case challenges the *ratio legis* by proposing a new, different, revolutionary *ratio*. All the extraordinary singularities that emerge in legal discourse today are epiphenomena of larger societal phenomena. Obviously, on the other hand, sometimes laws shape society—they are not simple mirrors of larger trajectories.

The extraordinary cases like *Brown* are self-referential, that is to say, they are unique but their uniqueness derives from the very process of their promotion as exemplary singularities. The force of the singularity is produced and legitimized by the "*sensus communis*", which is a very broad expression indicating a texture of relations, discourses and practices that make it the case for a singularity to acquire exemplary force. Alessandro Ferrara makes explicit reference to the *sensus communis* in all his works about exemplarity and he distinguishes two kinds of *sensus communis*: (i) on the one hand, the *sensus communis* can be defined from a phenomenological point of view as something contingent; (ii) on the other hand, the *sensus communis* can also be defined from a quasi-naturalist perspective. In a phenomenological sense, authors like Husserl and Schutz suggest to grasp *sensus communis* intersubjectively: there is a plurality of human actors and they all act in a common space. *Sensus communis* thus corresponds to a space inhabited by a community of people, and is basically a common space of interaction. It is a horizon that moves with the community that defines it.[46]

The relationship with the *sensus communis* and thus with the political community within which a singular case has been promoted *as* an exemplary case is crucial, because it can also hide the presence of specific interests and values.

---

46 Ferrara, (2008, 8 ff).

The underlying question is: what happens when exemplary cases are such because they have been chosen strategically to establish a principle that is believed to be just only by a certain group of individuals? In other words: if it is true that a singularity becomes exemplary when it represents better than other singularities a value that is widely accepted by the majority of people, what happens if a case is considered exemplary even though it does not represent the majority of opinions and inclinations or even though it is used strategically to validate a principle considered valuable only by a dominating group? When used strategically, the singular exemplary case embodies a modern political principle *against* a juridical principle.

The ordinary–extraordinary dichotomy can also be used for purposeful reasons, and it is on this aspect that I intend to focus in the present section. The use made of the extraordinary singularity appears clearly if we observe the legal domain, where the practice of "impact" or "strategic" litigation has become very popular during the 20th century and is widespread in fields of jurisprudence sensitive to public policies, such as for instance in the field of civil rights. Impact or strategic litigation is the practice of bringing a singular lawsuit to higher courts, and thus of making this lawsuit extraordinary and exemplary in the attempt to produce societal change. For instance, *Obergefell v. Hodges* (2015) is now considered a paradigm of the fight for equal rights for same-sex couples in particular for what concerns marriage. Such a litigation has had a crucial role in common law systems and in particular in the United States, where the importance of the singular case is an intrinsic characteristic of the juridical system (which is traditionally not the case in civil law systems, where abstract and general norms are usually the fundamental normative device), in particular in relation to themes like desegregation, abortion, and same-sex marriage.

In law, the emergence of a case as extraordinary and the consequent capacity that it has to produce effects on other cases has challenged the problem of the legitimacy and the validity of the sources of normativity. If general and abstract norms are usually legitimized by norms of a higher rank, a case is legitimized as "normative" by its own force and by more indeterminate and unspecified criteria, such as the *sensus communis*. For this reason, the use made of singular cases in terms of impact on litigations has been widely criticized both at the level of general theory of law (i); and at the level of the political legitimacy of these litigations (ii). In the first case (i), in countries with a constitutional separation of powers, political and social changes will usually be driven by reforms of the legal texts. Impact litigation goes against the traditional separation of powers because it is a jurisdictional body (a court) that produces a new model or norm. At the level of the political legitimacy of impact litigation (ii), a more thorough series of remarks is required. For instance, in the last few years there have been various decisions concerning homosexual parenting in Italy which have been considered as exemplary singular narratives that have contributed to define a new idea of marriage, parenting, and family. This series of individual decisions and rulings (among the others: Corte di Cassazione 19599/2016; Ordinanza Corte d'Appello Trento, 23/02/2017; Decreto Tribunale di Napoli, 11/11/2016—to mention just a few)[47] offers an interesting example of what it means to establish a general principle through the strategic use of singular (supposedly extraordinary) cases.

Let us observe the specific legal question at stake: why did the emergence of some cases as extraordinary create a debate in Italian public discourse? The process of their emergence is particularly interesting from the point of view of the different uses that can be made of the dichotomy ordinary–extraordinary: as a matter of fact, the extraordinary, groundbreaking and apparently innovative character of a certain decision (or of a group of decisions) can be used to argue that reforms of the juridical order are needed. And in order to do so, debates around the singular case can be fostered to make them appear extraordinary and illustrate the validity of the rhetorical arguments used by the judges in the decision. Thus, this series of cases is interesting because it shows that the extraordinary force of individual narratives can both emerge from the context and can be validated by the *sensus communis*, but it can also be constructed voluntarily by lobbies. All these cases (on homosexual parenting in Italy) concerned the possibility for same-sex couples to access the right to parenting. The recognition of this right for same-sex couples has been criticized by feminist intellectuals and jurists, since they claim that the cases were literally "used" to force the introduction of a neutral principle of equality between same-sex couples which they consider unjust. Those cases were chosen among others to be promoted as extraordinary, but (according to the critics) there was nothing really extraordinary in them. They were presented *as* such in order to overcome the ancient *regula iuris "mater semper certa"*, and thus in order to provide equal and neutral access to parenting for everyone. These singular conflicts were chosen to represent the values of those who believe that in civil and fundamental rights, neutrality is always the best solution: in other words, for those who claim that equality can be reached through neutrality.

According in particular to Silvia Niccolai,[48] these litigations are being used strategically (according to the practice of strategic litigations) in order to call into play an idea of law that must always create equality through the abolition of all differences between singular individuals and singular narratives.

47 Silvia Niccolai (2017).
48 Niccolai (2017).

Two approaches to law are conflicting in this frame: on the one hand, an approach for which all differences need to be broken down (this is the approach represented by the civil rights activists who *made* those cases extraordinary and who promoted them as such); on the other hand, an approach for which equality is not a mere algebraic calculation or a neutral concept, but is instead the product of experience and of a prudential approach in the balancing of values and interests (this is promoted in particular by Niccolai, who considers neutrality as a destruction of the principle of *différence* that has been central in all feminist fights for juridical recognition). Niccolai claims that the strategic use of singular cases works to the destroy the possibility to re-read the filiation in a non-neutral key, and precisely in a *feminine* way (according to the idea of *différence*). The cases are not extraordinary as such, but they are *created as extraordinary singularities* or presented as such in order to question the (partial and not neutral) rule "*mater semper certa*". In each extraordinary case, an archetypical struggle relives: the struggle between equality before the law, on the one hand, and equality as equity, fairness or reasonableness, on the other hand. The former states the creative, engineering and unlimited power of those who are in charge of governing a community; the latter aims at limiting the power of those who are in charge of governing a community by taking differences into account. This example should demonstrate that the difference between ordinary and extraordinary depends on the way the singularities are *used* in legal argumentation and is, in other words, directly related to the way legal rhetoric is used in public discourse. As already pointed out, in fact, singular cases can emerge as extraordinary according to the will of a group of interest, of lobbies, or of authorities that promote the recognition of some litigations as extraordinary in order to see them emerge, among others, as exemplary.

Each strategic litigation, by becoming exemplary and by being used as such, excludes other paths and other interpretations. Each one is an evocation of what Cass Sunstein defined as the "Anticaste principle", that tends to hide the fact that, in contemporary societies, the demand of justice might find different answers. To go back to the example analyzed by these feminist scholars, and in particular by Niccolai, recently we have seen a trend in Italy where individuals seeking recognition of peculiar rights interpellate judges as if they were legislators. Judges, following the wave of the current fights for civil rights (similarly to what had happened in the United States in the case of *Brown* in 1954), sometimes respond with their power by neutralizing the system in order to create equality among couples of all sexual orientations.

The extraordinary character of the case is a consequence of the fact that those cases destroy a precedent equilibrium in which the sexual difference was still recognized. The strategic character of the singular case is proved by the terms used to refer to these cases: "right to homo-parenting" ("*omogenitorialità*"), for example, indicates that through the individual litigation the groups of interest want to establish a new abstract norm, a new category of rights (thus showing that the existing categories do not cover the needs of guarantee that have emerged within society). This process of construction of a new category through the singularity parallels the construction of new artistic forms or genres in order to include extraordinary objects such as *Brillo Box* or *Fountain*. Though the cases are singular and particular, their narratives sound (or appear, or are treated as) universal.

Paradoxically, when singular instances are used as in the aforementioned strategic litigations for the recognition of new categories of rights, the extraordinary singularity is transformed into a means to reach a neutralization. Niccolai observes that the cases that were chosen for the strategic litigations were selected for their specific characteristics in order to make the argumentation easier. All of those cases involved lesbian couples, in order to show that same-sex couples are completely able to raise a child—two women, for the common sense, are better suited at raising a child than two men. Along these lines, singular cases can be used to contrast an ancient *regula* through their persuasive force and through this persuasion the singular—apparently extraordinary—cases lead to define a new general rule that subverts the traditional principle known as "*mater semper certa*". In this sense, the singular (extraordinary) litigations are used to affirm distributive justice in order to assert a new rule: the problem is that this procedure affirms law as mere *voluntas* and as a mere power-relation. This all demonstrates how singular court decisions can be used strategically to change the normative order: the judge becomes the substitute of the legislator who applies a principle of equality which corresponds to a neutralization of the natural and biological difference between man and woman, i.e., of gender differences.

Impact litigations are constructed around the extraordinary singularities that become symbols of a fight for the recognition of rights, but they are not reduced to the argumentation of the cases: public discourse is also permeated by claims of "equality" and "recognition." For instance, like in the case of homosexual parenting in Italy and in the fight for the step-child adoption, both of which participated in the construction of the symbolic value of the singular cases. At the same time, feminists who declared to be against these exemplary decisions were accused of being homophobic, conservative, and reactionary.

A similar process of construction and use of the extraordinary character of individual narratives can be seen in literature, where stories of individuals can be manipulated or, to use a word with a less negative connotation, can be constructed and presented as extraordinary: epic poetry is a paradigmatic field in this sense. Epic heroes are like nobody else: they are unique and their deeds are extraordinary. The ways in which their stories are told is part of this construction of their exemplarity. Literature, more than law and also more than figurative art, is in fact the art of writing, where the choice of what can be said and what is fictionally constructed, as well as the formal expedients used in the narration of the singular story, are crucial aspects of the literary technique. Literature shows how techniques of narration are a fundamental part of the use and the construction of the extraordinary starting from ordinary events, facts and proper names.

The case, in literature, is treated as an *hapax*: a unique occurrence that becomes a model, an exception to the ordinary course of life. The exemplary character, in literature, is fabricated by a series of factors: the function played by the specific case, how it is presented, described and archived, the reception it has in relation to the public discourse. This tension between ordinary and extraordinary is thus defined according to a complex series of factors and it is not just a characteristic of the singularity. To observe the construction of exemplarity does not mean to say that exemplarity is always artificial, but it means instead to recognize that there is always a case behind the example and that the *inscription as an exemplum* is what makes the singularity exemplary. This observation leads to an enlargement of the perspective on exemplarity that includes the singularity—the series of individual events and proper names that describe the content of the case—and the whole process and series of elements that promote the singularity to another level, the normative level of the norm embodied in the *exemplum*.

Peter Goodrich has recently gone back to the question of the importance of exemplary cases to specify the content of the norm: in order to explain the relationship between the abstract norm and the individual case, Goodrich uses the metaphor of an undressed body.[49] The abstract norm is like an undressed body, or an empty space, that needs its clothes and its furniture: the legal example is used in large part to dress the rule. A naked norm, for common lawyers, is simply an abstraction, a "nebulosity" that needs its particulars, its cases, to have meaning and to have an impact on jurisprudence and on legal knowledge. The individual case that interpellates the norm is not (just) the possibility of the concretization and of the application of the general and abstract norm, but it represents (also) the process of realization of the law. The singularity that interpellates the norm is the very meaning of the law.

In the frame of the general thesis underlying this book, the general norm is the order and the *exemplum* is the extraordinary. The *exemplum* is a kind of unforeseen, but it is the unforeseen without which the abstract norm would

49 Goodrich, (2018, 393–406).

remain an empty space, or indeed a naked body. The particular story, the particular event, gesture and life integrate the meaning of the general norm. Goodrich writes:

> At common law the rule exists only in its examples. There is no singular *exemplum* except as a momentary induction or, as used to be said illation from the mutable and inconstant series of *exempla*, the infinite particulars of a law made only through the instances of its casuistic application [...].
>
> GOODRICH 2018, 394

Conclusion

To conclude, I would like to go back to something I just mentioned here and there in text: in my opinion, casuistry indicates a fertile methodology to work on the intersections between law and society, and, from a disciplinary point of view, between law and humanities.

The mechanisms of generalization that stem from the extraordinary cases can unveil the processes of normalization that intrinsically characterize the law. Considering particular cases that touch upon complex juridical issues—that in their being extraordinary lead to define the limits between the search for a practical solution and the natural attitude of law to generalize—leads to consider the dichotomy, or opposition, between ordinary and extraordinary as the core of all juridical normativity, that is to say as the place of the encounter between factuality and normativity.

The singular cases can take the legal theorists out of the patterns of law, into a dimension where figuration, translation, and analogy play a very important—if not an essential—role. There, one can explore how legal knowledge functions, through a process that Yan Thomas has defined "*généralisation*", claiming that more than with mere generalisation, in the end what legal expertise deals with is the stabilisation of the extraordinary situations.[50]

By approaching normativity through the extraordinary singularities, the description of the ordinary and the stabilization of the exceptional become confused: they become one procedure and yet remain separate processes. The *cas extraordinaire* is a paradigmatic space of encounter of heterogeneous dimensions: first of all, the ordinary and the extraordinary and then, equally

---

50 Thomas (2005, 45 ff).

importantly, the legal and extra-legal. The need to incorporate the unexpected and the extraordinary challenges the order and leads to a redefinition of its *katechon*, of its limit.

Casuistry is a typical method used in the field of ethics: its goal is to derive general principles from clear-cut cases. Such a model can be useful when values or rules are in conflict, because it offers a solution to balance interests and not a general description of how the conflict might or should be resolved.

As mentioned before, the notion of exemplarity is based on an idea of validity that allows for the reconciliation of universalism and pluralism of cultures because it allows to settle conflicts of interests and of values in ways that are recognized as valid across the cultural divides that characterize contemporary societies. Exemplary cases and exemplary narratives both (and equally) have the capacity to speak to members of diverse political cultures. The purpose of their specificity is not to be exact, or to be perfectly coherent with respect to general norms. Their aim is to illustrate the importance of value, fairness, and justice—or conversely, of radical injustice, through the singular case. In fact, what contemporary societies demand of any conception of universal values—such as justice—is that they should be able to settle conflicts. Thus, what we can gain from the paradigmatic singularities is their capacity to bridge the differences among the diverse conceptions of the person, of human life, and of the values embedded in the various cultures.

Exemplary cases have a strong normative impact at a historical-political, cultural, and juridical level. They define the boundaries of the public debate around the main conflicts of contemporary juridical cultures. Litigations on extraordinary cases show the politicization of law more than positive norms. It is impossible to define a juridical culture in general terms, once and for all. This term, 'culture', when applied to law, is too broad and too complex, and it is virtually impossible to pin it down exactly. Exemplary cases embody a peculiar form of normativity embedded in the extra-legal reality, and yet they have an unquestionable political and juridical force.

Exemplary judgments embody the fundamental political and legal trends, and create a strong connection between ethics and law. They also influence the cultural horizon. On the one hand, they activate a form of legal consciousness, since they intercept problems common to a large number of subjects. On the other, exemplary cases can emerge as such only in the frame of a specific context. They stand at the threshold between juridical normativity and other sources of normativity. These cases embody a *momentum* from a historical-political, a cultural, and juridical point of view because they provoke "earthquakes" in the public domain by showing the conflicts between norms and values. The public impact of exemplary cases is particularly important because such cases regard private citizens' stories. The consequences that they produce, though originating in the private spheres, become universal.

To draw some conclusions valid for both parts of this essay, i.e. valid for both the artistic and the legal discourse, I will bullet point the main theses about the extraordinary singularity:

(i) as noted by Odo Marquard in *Defense of the Accidental*,[51] the case is what is not entirely impossible, nor entirely necessary; it could be otherwise, and could also not exist. It is interesting because it shows the contingency of normativity.

(ii) The perfect singularity always appears, or is described and presented, as in the case of impact-strategic litigations in law—as a potential infraction of the rules. It emerges as a new *ratio*. It is important that exemplary action is individual. The case, as Italian philosopher Enzo Melandri claimed,[52] has to be revolutionary. It must create some surprise-effect, like in Duchamp's *Fountain*.

(iii) The extraordinary case shows the possibility of what, until then, had been considered impossible. The extraordinary nature of the singular exemplary case is thus first and foremost a reaction to the ordinary: exemplary actions are reactions, they can only be exercised in the face of some resistance. As Maurizio Ferraris recalls in his book *Emergenza*, in the second letter to the Thessalonians (2 Thess 2,6–7), Paul speaks of κατέχον, "obstacle", in the neutral, or κατέχων, "he who is obstructive", in the male form—as is something or someone who keeps the Antichrist at bay. The case is the limit of the norm and also the possibility of its concretization.

(iv) When extraordinary, a case stands instead of (in place of) something else. It is an index. It represents values and principles that transcend it and yet it remains concrete, unique, imperfect and incomplete.

(v) The extraordinary creates a new "ordinary". Consider for instance the following series of cases: *Olmstead v. United States* (1928), *Katz v. United States* (1967), *Kyllo v. United States* (2001), *Jones v. United States* (2012). Progressively, they have redefined the relationship between public and private in American law through a series of singular stories that constituted exemplary cases and that redefined the concept of "privacy" in the American legal culture.

(vi) The extraordinary case shows the multiple values of the *ars rhetorica*: beyond argumentation and persuasion, the approach that I propose invites to consider rhetorics from the perspective of its multiple functions.

51 Marquard (1991).
52 Melandri (2004).

First and foremost, looking at juridical normativity from the perspective of the singularity invites to consider rhetorics as a field of production of knowledge and not only as a field of argumentation-justification. As Peter Goodrich notes in a recent essay,[53] according to James Boyd White (*The Legal Imagination*, 1973), rhetorics is a humanistic enterprise connected primarily to the classics and secondarily to literary criticism and poetics as devices for legal interpretation and for community building. Yet the real point made by Goodrich is that rhetorics signals—in site of its very diverse embodiments—the conjunction between the law and other disciplines. All figurative language in law and in all normative orders (thus in art as well) signals the interference of different discourses.

(vii) The force of the singularity is hence stronger in pluralist contexts (Ferrara): as it was the case in ancient Rome, when a stable system of rules encountered other systems of rules in the provinces, the contemporary era—dominated by multiple pluralist regimes—is especially characterized by the emergence of extraordinary singularities.

(viii) Once established as exemplary, the extraordinary singularity becomes a standard of interpretation—until the next extraordinary singularity. It establishes artistic genres and jurisprudential trends, as it was in the European Court of Justice case C-282/10 *Dominguez*, that was considered a standard for the balance between national law and European law. Or as it also was in the European Court of Human Rights case *Lautsi v. Italy*—30814/06, which ruled that the requirement in Italian law that crucifixes be displayed in classrooms of state schools does not violate the European Convention on Human Rights, thus creating a standard of interpretation for similar cases concerning freedom of religion within Europe.

(ix) The extraordinary case, once recognized as such, can work as a standard also outside the system in which it originated. One of the consequences of the extraordinary character of some specific cases is indeed that they might end up being used as standards or benchmarks also outside the system within which they were generated. For instance, the US Supreme Court is a very interesting example of a source of decisions that are "produced" in the American system and are applied immediately in that system, but whose echo and application go much further than that. In a way, it is a court that deals so much with the definition of the limits between ordinary and extraordinary, that it ends up being considered as an "exemplary" voice also outside the United States. So it happens, for instance, that the *European Coalition for Civil Rights and Liberties*, a platform of

53 Goodrich (2014).

human rights activists that follow human rights issues at a global level and that tries to provide updated reports of human rights policies that will have an impact also at a European level,[54] follows the jurisprudence of the American Supreme Court and announces the discussions of the cases that are already or will become (very likely) standards of interpretation also outside the United States. It happened with the discussion of the case *Carpenter v. United States*, that has redefined the standards of the expectation of privacy under the Fourth Amendment. While I am writing, *Carpenter* is still a "pending case" before the Supreme Court: it raises the question of whether the government violates the Fourth Amendment of the United States Constitution by accessing—without a valid warrant—the historical cell phone location records of an individual. The decision is expected to clarify the Fourth Amendment's influence upon the ability of law enforcement agencies to obtain smartphone data collected by third-party communication providers. After the scandal of Cambridge Analytica and Facebook, the wait is amplified.

(x) The extraordinary singularity is an allegory: a symbolic narrative that conveys a meaning not explicitly set forth in the narrative. The allegorical attitude of the extraordinary case makes it possible for different levels of meaning to converge in the singularity in which the individual narrative stands for something not directly or explicitly stated.

(xi) Because of its capacity to represent a discourse or system of values broader than the singularity, thus because of its allegorical nature, the case always involves an interpretive process and invites a re-discussion of the content of norms, of their limits and future uses.

(xii) Because of its allegorical nature, the case is also the place where the narratives that characterize a determined culture in a given historical context emerge: it is a surface where multiple needs, desires and fights emerge or re-emerge. As shown by the original embodied norm, Christ, each gesture—each detail—characterizing the singularity can refer to another level of meaning. The merging of *allos* (other) and *agoreuein* (to speak in public) produces the sense of "other-speaking". The singular case that is promoted at the level of an extraordinary case has at least a double meaning: the surface, and the result of the allegorical interpretation. It is not by chance that the Latin term *allegoria* was used as a synonym of *symbolon*, the encoded manifestation of transcendental meaning—both remote and immediate. As a privileged object of study of poststructuralist theory, and of Paul de Man's in particular, the allegory—understood

54 https://cild.eu/blog/2017/11/29/la-corte-suprema-americana-e-la-privacy-nellera-digitale/.

as the figure of the double or plural meanings—has become the paradigmatic instance of rhetorics, and the sign whose meaning cannot be fixed but is continually deferred, both calling for and resisting interpretation.

(xiii) Understood as the space of interpretation, and of intersection between different codes and different systems of values, the case can become the space of critical practice both in art and in law.

The multiplication of exemplary cases and of unique instantiations of individuality, as well as the repetition of the quotidian, defines the artistic and legal tradition. The singular cases are thus the *habitus* (in Latin terms) of both art and law: they constitute these two cultural domains, their sets of traditions, trends, paradigms, and standards—as well as their respective changes. The *habitus* is a form of life that is present in front of the rule, so the term illustrates what the case usually does with its interpellation of the norm through its concrete characters and through its extraordinary position in relation to the abstract order. The order, in fact, is abstract but it is in the potentiality of its concrete application in the individual case that the order has its *raison d'être*.

The empty space of the norm is filled—case by case—with the iteration of specific and contingent judgements which then constitute momentary and contextual examples. The norm needs to be "translated" to become real. The *exemplum*, the extraordinary case—is the *realization* of normativity. Without the possibility of the extraordinary interpellation and thus of the singularity that gets promoted into a norm, the law is like a naked sovereign: a concept in need of a symbolic system to support it. Goodrich writes:

> The King is only King in his clothes, as Louis Marin famously pointed out, and the same is true of the juridicity of the sovereign. The *exempla* are not bodies but clothes, or more precisely habit in all its diverse armorial, heraldic, suited, enrobed and decorous forms. The sovereign is the *exemplum*, precisely because the sovereign is hidden, a secret, an empty space of auratic transmission, or in Hobbes' terms, an angel, which is to say an idea without body, all feathers, all clothes […].
>
> GOODRICH 2018, 393 ff

He then recalls Legendre, who claimed that it is human to veil the void: the extraordinary is thus what gives flesh and blood to the ordinary.[55] The exemplary case is what attributes sense to the abstract norm: it is the life that enters the law and "activates" it. The empty space of the norm is filled in by the *exemplum*. Interestingly, the *exemplum* activates a circularity: if, on the one hand, it

55 Legendre (2007, 52–54).

gives "concreteness" to the general and abstract norm, on the other hand the *exemplum* is itself an empty space, a *medium* that can convey different values and discourses. Singular, extraordinary cases give meaning to abstract norms and principles and, at the same time, they are empty signifiers, blank spaces, schemes that allow for the assertion of diverse values and social necessities. For example, the paradigmatic case *Lautsi v. Italy* (European Court of Human Rights, 2011) established that the requirement in Italian law that crucifixes be displayed in classrooms of schools does not violate the European Convention on Human Rights. Such a principle was brought in the European legal system through the singular case.

Thinking about art and law through the relation between the ordinary and the extraordinary reveals the characteristics that these two fields have in common. As perfectly shown by Passeron and Revel in their work on the case, two essential features are always present in the qualification of an occurrence as a "case". The first is the obstacle that the singularity of a situation opposes to the habitual movement of perception or with the application of already codified norms of explanatory or prescriptive discourse.[56] The second is the fact that a singularity can be called a "case" only if the history from which it derives and of which it is a product has valued the circumstances that make *that* case different from other cases. Pluralist normative orders such as art and law, today, require a new rhetorical approach and the foundation of a new casuistry. The renewal of ethical casuistry and of juridical analysis of cases that I propose in this essay leads to a questioning of the exclusive domination exercised by the hypothetico-deductive model and the universalist paradigms on all the operations of inference and of proof in social and human sciences.

In its incomplete perfection, the extraordinary singularity is creative and porous. Through its pores, repressed forces can emerge in a revolutionary—and sometimes purposeful and strategic—way. But revolutions cost. Enzo Melandri, in his book *La linea e il circolo* (1968), concludes that the use of singularities can be either good or bad. In any case, we always refer to singular cases and we always draw analogies between singularities when trying to understand, or change, a general norm. On the very last page of his work, he invites the reader to look for analogies between cases and to look for new paradigms: sometimes it might feel like looking for a needle in a haystack. And yet, he calls for a philosophy of the needle, and not of the haystack. I welcome his suggestion and conclude on the ambiguity of the relationship between ordinary and extraordinary. More specifically, on the risks of a use of extraordinary cases without a theory about their emergence and about their nature. In a scene

56 Passeron and Revel (2005).

of the film *Jesus Christ Superstar* (1973), released the same year as White's *The Legal Imagination*, a fat and all-dressed-up King Herod dances surrounded by drag queens. He sings at Jesus, who stands serious, scared, and bewildered in front of him:

> Jesus, I am overjoyed to meet you face to face.
> [encounter between the order and the extraordinary][57]
> You've been getting quite a name all around the place.
> [affirmation of the case as a "norm"]
> Healing cripples, raising from the dead.
> [extraordinary deeds and actions]
> And now I understand you're God,
> At least, that's what you've said.
> So, you are the Christ, you're the great Jesus Christ.
> Prove to me that you're divine; change my water into wine.
> That's all you need do, then I'll know it's all true.
> [verification of the validity of the case as a norm]
> Come on, King of the Jews.
> Jesus, you just won't believe the hit you've made around here.
> You are all we talk about, the wonder of the year.
> Oh what a pity if it's all a lie.
> Still, I'm sure that you can rock the cynics if you tried.
> So, you are the Christ, you're the great Jesus Christ.
> Prove to me that you're no fool; walk across my swimming pool.
> If you do that for me, then I'll let you go free.
> Come on, King of the Jews.
> I only ask what I'd ask any superstar.
> What is it that you have got that puts you where you are?
> [problem of the origin and emergence of the extraordinary singularity]
> I am waiting, yes I'm a captive fan.
> I'm dying to be shown that you are not just any man.
> [the singularity must be unique, otherwise it remains the whatever case]
> So, if you are the Christ, yes the great Jesus Christ
> Feed my household with this bread.
> You can do it on your head.
> Or has something gone wrong. Jesus, why do you take so long?

57 The comments into brackets are mine, the lyrics correspond to the original text written by Tim Rice.

> [interpellation of the norm towards the case: is it really valid? What legitimizes it?]
> Oh come on, King of the Jews.
> Hey! Aren't you scared of me Christ?
> Mr. Wonderful Christ?
> You're a joke. You're not the Lord.
> You are nothing but a fraud.
> [the risk, the cost, of the revolutionary attitude of the case]

This long excerpt is particularly meaningful for me, since this musical has been very present, for different reasons, in my life. Also, I have always found the image of King Herod interpellating Jesus Christ very touching, in a way which is not common. It is not the trial, it's before it: the image shows the possibility of the judgment but it is still a more informal conversation, and in some sense it proves that the judgement could have been avoided. It's not the physical punishment nor the crucifixion, but potentially it already brings the fear of the (temporary) defeat of the project of Christendom. The embodied norm remains silent, he is as if naked in front of the provocation of the authority. Who is he? Why do people follow him? His silence could be his choice not to open the communication with Herod, but it could also represent the emptiness and the nakedness of the norm described by Peter Goodrich. Between ordinary and extraordinary, both in art and law, there is a void.

Bibliography

Adajian, Thomas. 2016. "The Definition of Art", *The Stanford Encyclopedia of Philosophy.* https://plato.stanford.edu/archives/sum2016/entries/art-definition/.

Andina, Tiziana. 2017. *What is Art? The Question of Definition Reloaded.* Leiden: Brill Research Perspectives in Art and Law. (1.2) 1–88.

Andina, Tiziana. 2018. "Exemplarity in Contemporary Arts". *Law & Literature* 3 (eds. Angela Condello and Alessandro Ferrara) (3) 407–420.

Ando, Clifford. 2015. "Exemplum, Analogy, and Precedent in Roman Law". *Exemplarity and Singularity. Thinking through Particulars in Philosophy, Literature, and Law* (eds. Michèle Lowrie and Susanne Lüdemann). New York: Routledge. 111–122.

Auerbach, Eric. (1946) 2003. *Mimesis: The Representation of Reality in Western Literature.* Princeton: Princeton University Press.

Cassirer, Ernst. 1923. *Philosophie der symbolischen Formen. Erster Teil: Die Sprache.* Berlin: Bruno Cassirer. Translated as *The Philosophy of Symbolic Forms. Volume One: Language.* New Haven: Yale University Press, 1955.

Cassirer, Ernst. (1925a) 1953. *Language and Myth*. New York: Dover Publications.

Cassirer, Ernst. 1925b. *Philosophie der symbolischen Formen. Zweiter Teil: Das mythische Denken*. Berlin: Bruno Cassirer. Translated as *The Philosophy of Symbolic Forms. Volume Two: Mythical Thought*. New Haven: Yale University Press, 1955.

Cavell, Stanley. 1981. *Pursuits of Happiness: The Hollywood Comedy of Remarriage*, Cambridge: Cambridge University Press.

Condello, Angela and Terrone, Enrico. 2017. "Genre Classification: A Problem of Normativity and Exemplarity". *Law and the Arts. Elective Affinities and Relationships of Tension* (eds. Gephart, Werner and Leko, Jure). Frankfurt: Klostermann. 39–46.

Condello, Angela. 2018. "Exemplarity: Story, Time and Gesture of a Threshold". *Law & Literature* (eds. Angela Condello and Alessandro Ferrara) (3) 421–432.

Condello, Angela and Mason, Luke. 2019. "Make it New! The Redeeming Modernism of Law and the Collapsing of its Polarities". *Polemos. Journal of Law, Literature and Culture*. 1/2019.

Cover, Robert. 1984. "The Supreme Court, 1982 Term—Foreword: Nomos and Narrative". Harvard Law Review (97) 4–68.

Currie, Gregory. 2004. *Arts and Minds*. Oxford: Oxford University Press.

Danto, Arthur. 1992. *Beyond the Brillo Box: The Visual Arts in Post-historical Perspective*. New York: Farrar Straus Giroux.

Delacroix, Sylvie. 2006. *Legal Norms and Normativity. An Essay in Genealogy*. Oxford: Hart Publishing.

Ferrara, Alessandro. 2008. *The Force of the Example. Explorations in the Paradigm of Judgement*. New York: Columbia University Press.

Ferraris, Maurizio. 2016. *Emergenza*. Torino: Einaudi.

Fleming, Paul. 2009. *Exemplarity and Mediocrity. The Art of the Average from Bourgeois Tragedy to Realism*. Stanford: Stanford University Press.

Foucault, Michel. 1988. "Practicing criticism". *Michel Foucault: Politics Philosophy, Culture Interviews and Other Writings 1977–1984* (ed. Lawrence Kritzman). New York: Routledge.

Fraade, Steven. 2005. "Nomos and Narrative Before Nomos and Narrative". *Yale Journal of Law & the Humanities*, (17) 81–96.

Geach, Peter. 1972. *Logical Matters*. Berkeley: University of California Press.

Goodrich, Peter. 2014. "Rhetoric and Modern Law". *Oxford Handbook of Rhetorical Studies* (ed. Michael MacDonald). Oxford: Oxford Handbooks online (Print version: November 2017).

Goodrich, Peter. 2018. "The Example of Undressing. Obnubilations on the Empty Space of the Rule". *Law & Literature* 3 (eds. Angela Condello and Alessandro Ferrara) (3) 393–406.

Harvey, Irene E. 2002. *Labyrinths of Exemplarity. At the Limits of Deconstruction*. New York: State University of New York Press.

Hollander, Dana. 2008. *Exemplarity and Chosenness. Rosenzweig and Derrida on the Nation of Philosophy*. Stanford: Stanford University Press.

Kripke, Saul A. 1980. *Naming and Necessity*. Cambridge: Harvard University Press.

Kuhn, Thomas. 1962. *The Structure of the Scientific Revolutions*. Chicago: University of Chicago Press.

Langlands, Rebecca. 2015. "Roman exemplarity: mediating between general and particular". *Exemplarity and Singularity. Thinking through Particulars in Philosophy, Literature, and Law* (eds. Michèle Lowrie and Susanne Lüdemann). New York: Routledge. 68–80.

Legendre, Pierre. 2007. *Dominium mundi: L'empire du management*. Paris: Mille et Une Nuits.

Manderson, Desmond. 2012. "Modernism, Polarity, and the Rule of Law". *Yale Journal of Law & Humanities*. (24) 475–505.

Margolis, Joseph. 2010. "The Importance of Being Earnest about the Definition and Metaphysics of Art". *The Journal of Aesthetics and Art Criticism*. (68: 3) 215–223.

Margolis, Joseph. 2010. *The Cultural Space of the Arts and the Infelicities of Reductionism*. New York: Columbia University Press, 2010.

Marquard, Odo. (1986) 1991. *In Defense of the Accidental*. Oxford: Oxford University Press.

Mazzoni, Guido. (2011) 2017. *Theory of the Novel*. Translated by Zakiya Hanafi. Cambridge, MA: Harvard University Press.

Melandri, Enzo. (1968) 2004. *La linea e il circolo*. Studio logico-filosofico sull'analogia. Macerata: Quodlibet.

Möller, Melanie. 2015. "Exemplum and Exceptio: building blocks for a rhetorical theory of the exceptional case". Translated by Jake Fraser. *Exemplarity and Singularity. Thinking through Particulars in Philosophy, Literature, and Law* (eds. Michèle Lowrie and Susanne Lüdemann). New York: Routledge. 96–110.

Niccolai, Silvia. 2017. "Diamo alla maternità quel che le spetta". *Maternità filiazione genitorialità. I nodi della maternità surrogata in una prospettiva costituzionale* (eds. Silvia Niccolai and Elisa Olivito). Napoli: Jovene. 191–234.

Passeron, Jean-Claude and Revel, Jacques (eds.). 2005. *Penser par cas*. Paris: EHESS.

Parry, Richard. 2014. "Ancient Ethical Theory". *The Stanford Encyclopedia of Philosophy* https://plato.stanford.edu/archives/fall2014/entries/ethics-ancient/.

Strawson, Peter. 1959. *Individuals: Essay in Descriptive Metaphysics*. London: Methuen.

Strawson, Peter. 1962. "Freedom and Resentment", reprinted in *Freedom and Resentment and Other Essays*. London: Methuen (1974). 1–28.

Strawson, Peter. 1966. *The Bounds of Sense: An Essay on Kant's Critique of Pure Reason*. London: Methuen.

Strawson, Peter. 1979. "Perception and its Objects", *Perception and Identity: Essays Presented to A. J. Ayer* (ed. Macdonal, G. F.). London: Macmillan. 41–60.

Terrone, Enrico. 2018. "Be Like This. Norms, Examples, Documents and Indexicals from a Neo-Aristotelian Perspective", *Law & Literature* 3 (eds. Angela Condello and Alessandro Ferrara) (3) 433–448.

Thévenin, Pierre. 2017. Le monde sur mésure. Une archéologie juridique des faits. Paris: Garnier.

Thomas, Yan. 2005. "L'extrême et l'ordinaire. Remarques sur le cas médiéval de la communauté disparue". *Penser par cas* (eds. Passeron, Jean-Claude and Revel, Jacques) 45–73.

Toracca, Tiziano. 2018. "Towards Exemplarity: When the Particular Matters". *Law & Literature* 3 (eds. Angela Condello and Alessandro Ferrara) (3) 449 ff.

Walton, Kendall. 1970. "Categories of Art". *Philosophical Review*. (79) 334–367.

www.ingramcontent.com/pod-product-compliance
Lightning Source LLC
Chambersburg PA
CBHW031333230926
51848CB00001B/217